Trapped Behind Enemy Lines

Trapped Behind Enemy Lines

*Accounts of British Soldiers and
their Protectors in the Great War*

John Anderson
Victor Piuk

Pen & Sword
MILITARY

First edition published in Great Britain in 2015 by
PEN AND SWORD MILITARY
an imprint of
Pen and Sword Books Ltd
47 Church Street, Barnsley
South Yorkshire S70 2AS

ISBN 978 1 47383 801 7

Printed and bound in England by
CPI Group (UK) Ltd, Croydon, CR0 4YY

Typeset in Times by CHIC GRAPHICS

Pen & Sword Books Ltd incorporates the imprints of
Archaeology, Atlas, Aviation, Battleground, Discovery,
Family History, History, Maritime, Military, Naval, Politics,
Railways, Select, Social History, Transport, True Crime,
Claymore Press, Frontline Books, Leo Cooper, Praetorian Press,
Remember When, Seaforth Publishing and Wharncliffe.

For a complete list of Pen and Sword titles please contact
Pen and Sword Books Limited
47 Church Street, Barnsley, South Yorkshire, S70 2AS, England
E-mail: enquiries@pen-and-sword.co.uk
Website: www.pen-and-sword.co.uk

Contents

Prologue

We arrived in the centre of Etaples on a dull August morning, excited by the anticipation of a great hunt and the hope of finding something interesting at the town's *brocante*. The word does not translate exactly into English, but a *brocante* is a cross between an antiques fair, a flea market and a car boot sale. You can come away with anything, or nothing. This French town on the Channel coast, which had accommodated thousands of soldiers during the Great War, was today in carnival mood. The place had hosted an infamous training establishment described by Wilfred Owen as: 'A vast, dreadful encampment. It seemed neither France nor England, but a kind of paddock where the beasts are kept a few days before the shambles.' Many thousands are here still, in the massive Commonwealth War Graves cemetery nearby, men who died of wounds or illness so close to home. Looking at the crush of stall holders and bargain hunters today there was a resemblance to a shambles, but the only terror here was the fear of a lost sale or of missing out on a long sought after collectable.

The *brocante* filled the town square and surrounding streets with stall after stall of old and interesting bric-à-brac, antiques and general second hand goods in bewildering variety. The French recycle their possessions with typical Gallic flair and enjoy explaining in great detail the provenance of anything in which one may have expressed an interest. They will happily take the first asking price with a smile, but bartering with them is a skill worth developing, even though they will make you feel as though you are taking food from the mouths of their children.

Still in darkness and with storm clouds gathering, we had dragged ourselves out of the sleeping bags in our caravan at half past four in the morning – or 0430 hrs by the military clock. Whichever was used it was still a shock! I had not realized there were two half past fours on the clock until we discovered the joy of *brocantes*. Canny folk, the French – they advertise the start time as eight, but if you get there fifteen minutes before that you are still two hours behind the dealers. However, we knew the ropes as veterans of many a *brocante* and so got there at six, when some of the stallholders were still setting up by torchlight.

We have a system: a quick whizz around, looking at the larger and more obvious items on offer, then a more thorough sortie as it begins to get light, checking out the contents of the many boxes and cases. It was towards the end of our first tour that my good lady Kath spoke, saying: 'Go and have a look at that, it's got *Daily Telegraph* written on it.' Dutifully, I threaded my way through and over the array of goods on offer and strategically placed to make it impossible to reach the object of my interest. The dealer had laid a tarpaulin on the uneven footpath and spread out his wares: china and glass collectables to the front, books and pictures at the sides on rickety folding tables, small items of furniture of an unknown vintage and the inevitable table by which the dealer stood tearing lumps from his breakfast baguette; uncovered slices of ham and cheese were being stuffed into the bread, and it was all being washed down with the first glass of rosé of the day.

As he watched me precariously tiptoe my way through and around his goods he drained his glass, re-lit his cheroot and got to me just as I picked the item up. His sales pitch chattered like a Maxim gun and I picked up only a few of the words of the French he fired at me. 'It is very beautiful and extremely rare,' he extolled, 'perhaps even unique.' The writing was all in English and I wondered if in reality he understood what he had. It was a certificate of some sort, backed by card, and it had clearly been displayed in a frame at some time, as the old mount was still in place around it. My first impression was that it was not print but beautifully handcrafted calligraphy and decoration. I read it and asked how much. He announced his price, but I did not need to barter on this occasion as he kindly offered me a discount during the pause while I worked out how to ask for one. He was kind enough to place the item in a large plastic bin liner, and as we walked away the first few drops of rain began to fall, steadily increasing to a heavy downpour. We ducked into the nearest café and looking back we noticed that our dealer was continuing with his breakfast, sheltering beneath a parasol and making no attempt to protect his stock from the pouring rain. It was only much later in the day, when we returned to the security of our touring van, that we fully realized what it was we had bought and how close it had come to being soaked and destroyed by the deluge.

As we read through the beautifully handwritten text we marvelled at the skill of the calligrapher and his or her careful attention to detail in the document's decoration, which included the Tricolour, the Union Flag and the regimental badge of the Scottish Rifles. The text read:

This Testimonial was presented to Madame Julie Celestine Baudhuin by the Lord Mayor of London at the Mansion House, on April 8, 1927 on behalf of a large number of readers of the *Daily Telegraph* who, deeply stirred by the story of the superb courage with which she succoured a British soldier at the risk of her own life in the Great War, subscribed for the purchase of an annuity as a token of the honour due from the British people to a brave Frenchwoman. Disdaining danger, Madame Baudhuin provided food and shelter for a prolonged period to a soldier cut off in the enemy lines, and suffered a cruel punishment from the invader for her courage and self-sacrifice. Wherever the wonderful story has been told it has excited the deepest and the purest emotions, and the subscribers to the annuity have been spontaneously moved to offer with their thanks and their admiration this testimonial of their earnest desire for her well-being and of their pride at being able to shew their appreciation of her rare magnanimity, her unflinching bravery during the years that the invader remained on her hearth, and her womanly loving-kindness to one whom her devotion saved.

Underneath this was written, *'1914 The Great War 1918'*.

Reading through this brought numerous questions to mind. Who was this Madame Baudhuin? Who was the soldier? How, why and when did he become cut off in the enemy lines? What happened to him, and what was the cruel punishment this mystery woman had suffered from the invader? The more we read and re-read the testimonial the more questions seemed to be raised. The Armistice of 11 November 1918 had ended the fighting, yet this testimonial was presented to Madame Baudhuin in April of 1927, almost nine years after the guns had fallen silent and the survivors began to return to their homes. Why so long? Clearly the *Daily Telegraph* and its readers were an important part of the story, but why? There were so many questions, and sitting in our caravan in the Somme village of Authuille we had no way of finding any of the answers – or so we thought.

Over the next few days we proudly showed the testimonial to a number of friends in the area who share our interest in history and in the Great War in particular. Each commented on its quality and agreed that it would be very interesting to find the answers to the many questions, but it was Kath who came up with the first clue. She asked, 'Can you remember reading a book called *A Foreign Field?* That was about soldiers trapped behind enemy lines during the First World War.' As luck would have it we had a copy in the caravan and, amazingly, there it was: a brief mention of a Frenchwoman called Madame Baudhuin from Le Cateau who had protected a young soldier of the 1st Battalion the Scottish Rifles (The Cameronians) by the name of David Cruickshank. So the first part of the puzzle was in place, but we could not have begun to imagine the story that was to unfold as other elements of the mystery were uncovered and pieced together.

During the course of my early research into David Cruickshank I contacted the regimental museum of the Cameronians and had a long chat with Terry Mackenzie, who was very helpful. He sent me copies of a couple of pages from *The Covenanter*, their regimental magazine, and copies of two articles in French. I had the documents translated and the story began to unfold. Not long after, I was invited to write a short piece for Tom Morgan's *Hellfire Corner* website. A few weeks after the piece went on line I received an e-mail. The sender was Glen Cruickshank, David's grandson. He had googled the name of his grandmother and found the piece. Now we had the nucleus of the story and a close family contact. But as anyone who has been bitten by the inquisitive bug knows, the more you find out the more you want to know, and one question just leads to another. It was, perhaps bizarrely, over a couple of acoustic guitars that the idea of writing this book was suggested – both its authors are keen amateur musicians as well as professional historians and guides living on the Somme battlefields. Between songs we began discussing the testimonial, which by now was framed and hanging on the wall of the room we were playing in. Then the idea emerged: how about teaming up to get really stuck into trying to find out as much as we could and writing a book? If we found it so intriguing, surely others would too? Little did we know that ahead of us were almost two years of research, reading, visits to archives and poring over documents and photographs – all very enjoyable, but time-consuming. Many a time the guitars had to take second place to the laptops. But here we are. We got there in the end.

This is chiefly the story of David Cruickshank, but also that of Patrick Fowler, Herbert Hull and a number of other British soldiers who found themselves helpless, frightened and trapped behind enemy lines during the retreat from Mons, the first clash between the British and German armies in 1914. It is a story of danger and fear, betrayal and tragedy, evasion and capture; for some it ends in front of a firing squad, for others there is love and triumph. Without the help of their French saviours it is probable that all these fugitive British soldiers would have been incarcerated for the duration of the war or would have perished. Many endured long periods on the run and suffered great hardships before being taken in by brave local villagers, who made great sacrifices for them and took tremendous risks on behalf of themselves and their loved ones. Not all made it through to the end of the war, despite the courage of heroic French men and women, who put their lives on the line time and time again, following the voice of their conscience during those desperate years in the clutches of their invaders.

Those who gave so much mostly found themselves forgotten relatively quickly after the 'war to end all wars' – but not completely. The illuminated scroll found in such fortunate circumstances on that August morning in the early twenty-first century was evidence of a remarkable story which has gone virtually untold for nearly 100 years; we will now tell it in depth for the first time. We are not attempting to write a history of the First World War – there are plenty of those at the moment, as we currently mark the centenary of the conflict – but there are elements of our story which refer to what was happening on a wider stage, as opposed to the restricted environment in which those trapped men and their saviours lived. Those events at all times shaped what was happening in these occupied communities behind enemy lines.

The men and women who endured those momentous times may have passed on, but their endeavours survive to inspire us. Many of the locations can still be visited, from the houses where some of the soldiers were hidden to, sadly, the graves of those who were betrayed and executed. Their stories deserve to be better known, and we hope that through this book more people may learn of their steadfastness, devotion and courage.

John Anderson and Victor Piuk
Longueval and Hardecourt aux Bois
December 2014

Chapter 1

Beginnings

The Chinese have a saying, 'May you live in interesting times', and the life of David Cruickshank could not fit the bill better if it tried. He experienced war, a near-fatal encounter, escape, love, jealousy, betrayal, capture, a trial for his life ending in a death sentence, a passionate call for mercy and then imprisonment, before achieving a bitter-sweet freedom. All of this took place in foreign tongues and far from his native land. Mix in a spell of enforced transvestism and it makes for a heady brew which might cause even the most imaginative novelist to blanch. But this was David's life before he had even reached his mid-twenties. Many remarkable stories have emerged from what we now call the First World War (initially known in its aftermath as the Great War), but there can surely be few as incredible as this.

David Cruickshank was born in Glasgow on 28 December 1894, but his father, William, had been born in 1868 150 miles away in Dufftown, Banffshire, on the banks of the River Spey, a town famed for having the greatest concentration of whisky distilleries in the land. Given whisky's importance to the local economy it should come as no surprise that William had worked as a distillery cooper since leaving school, a skilled trade carrying considerable status. On 18 July 1890 William married Annie Waddell, who hailed from Perth, over 100 miles away. But this was not the only big change in his life, because the marriage took place in Glasgow. The 1891 census recorded the couple living at 300 Charles Street in the Townhead area of the city. There were no children listed at this time, but this was to soon change.

What caused William to up sticks and move to Glasgow is unknown. Perhaps he fancied the change of pace which came with city life and the opportunity of better wages which often went hand in hand with it. As a newly married man, with a family soon to follow, more money was perhaps needed. Maybe there was a streak of adventure in him, something which would certainly be shared by his second-born son when he came along shortly afterwards. Let us hope William's wages did increase, for by the time of David's birth there were three young mouths to feed at home, with sister Isabella having been born three years earlier and brother William two years after that.

By the time of the 1911 census the Cruickshank family had grown further. Isabella was now nineteen, William seventeen and David sixteen, but they had been joined by several siblings: Harriet was fourteen, Hendry ten, Jeannie eight, youngest brother Frank six, and there was a baby of two months who was named after her mother. To provide for his brood William was still employed as a cooper, but now at a paint works. Annie was at home looking after the family but Isa, as the family called Isabella, also worked – as a shirt machinist. Her wage would have been sorely needed by such a large household, and no doubt the older girls would also have helped to look after their younger siblings. Two other wages, undoubtedly also welcome, were also coming in now, for William was working as a rivet heater while David was employed by the cleansing department of Glasgow Corporation. There had also been a change of address, which was now given as 4 Cobden Street, still in the city but in the Springburn area.

At this time the British Empire was at its height and much of that power and prestige was supplied by Glasgow. This major city was founded many centuries before as a fishing settlement on the banks of a river soon called the Clyde, and now most its wealth came from engineering, textiles, shipbuilding and allied trades along its banks. Its inhabitants were known as hard-working, shrewd and skilled. The population quintupled over the course of the nineteenth century to reach half a million. Among those arrivals were William and Annie Cruickshank. But despite the city's wealth, this great expansion had also resulted in poverty. The 1861 Census recorded 94 per cent of the population as working class. Massive overcrowding saw entire families, often themselves large, packed into single rooms in tenement blocks. But enlightened city government through the second half of the century brought massive changes for the better, and as the century drew to its end the Cruikshanks would benefit from many of these advances. Its council claimed Glasgow was now the best run city in the Empire.

A major industry of the period was the railway, and Glasgow's engineering expertise had been perfectly placed to capitalize on the 'railway fever' which developed throughout the world; soon locally built locomotives, rolling stock, girders and bridges were being shipped across the globe. In 1903 three major firms merged to form the North British Locomotive Company, employing 8,000 people in Glasgow, and in 1913 it did business worth £16 million. From its Springburn works a regular spectacle was the sight of completed engines being hauled away to Finnieston Quay for export all over the planet, something which never failed to draw a massive audience.

Springburn was now home to the Cruikshanks, and David, too, must have marvelled at this age and shared the confidence which caused many to call their town 'the second city of the Empire'. But for those looking deeper, there were clouds on the horizon of this apparently perfect world. Trade suffers recessions, with winners and losers. While iron and coal saw boom times during industrialization, more traditional hand-worked trades went to the wall. People awaited better times, sure that the grit and entrepreneurial skill of their city would see things improve again. And generally things did. The early twentieth century brought new challenges, though. Steam engines were giving way to those powered by oil, and these were not being built on the Clyde but in Germany. In 1913 the Clyde could still boast that one in three British ships was being built there, a total of 757,000 tonnes, but Germany's yards, with 646,000 tonnes, were closing the gap. Steel investment had been slow and some felt that laurels had been rested on too long and new drive and initiative were now lacking. But generally confidence in the present situation was high; the belief was that any potential problems would be overcome and progress would continue to be the regular pattern of life.

This was David Cruickshank's world as he left school aged fifteen and the twentieth century moved into its second decade. David gained the Leaving Certificate, showing he had reached a certain standard in a range of subjects. By the economic ranking of the day, his family was working class – as was 91 per cent of the city according to the 1901 Census. There was, however, a hierarchy within this broad classification. David's father was a skilled tradesman, and there was often an aspiration among skilled workers to see their lives and those of their families improve. This had already been demonstrated when the Cruikshanks moved to Glasgow from Speyside. Whether William wanted his boys to continue in education – and if they did themselves or had the capability – is unknown. William junior had already been working for two years by the time his younger brother came to leave school. It was anyway not common for working class families to send off their sons to university at this time.

So David went to work and, as seen earlier, the 1911 Census has him in the employ of the local authority's cleansing department. This covered a multitude of responsibilities and tasks and could have seen David engaged in jobs like sweeping litter and horse dung from the streets or moving refuse. There would probably have been initial excitement in being away from his school desk and in the real adult world, mixed perhaps with pride at being able to contribute to his family's upkeep; but the monotonous reality of this dull and dirty job must have eventually become wearing. The wages would have been modest for such unskilled work, and David would have had little to line his pockets with by the end of the week.

The Cruikshanks' little corner of the world in Springburn was dominated not only by the burgeoning locomotive works. Nearby was another massive building which might possibly also have had a considerable bearing on David's thoughts and actions in 1914. Maryhill Barracks was built in 1872, ironically enough after pressure on the government by Glasgow City Council, David's future employers, for a stronger military presence due to fear of growing 'riot and tumult' among the inhabitants of the industrial districts who were no strangers to protest and violence. Over four years a state-of-the-art barracks was built on a 12-hectare site which would be able to accommodate a regiment of infantry, a cavalry squadron and a battery of artillery. It was designated as the depot of the Highland Light Infantry, although it was used by many other regiments too, and such was its size it almost gave the feeling of a garrison town to the area, complete with military-titled pubs in the immediate locality such as the Elephant and Bugle, named after the design of the regimental badge.

So the regular sight of soldiers would have been nothing unusual to the young and perhaps impressionable David. Despite the description of Tommy Atkins, as the common British soldier was known from the writings and poetry of the immensely popular Rudyard Kipling, as little more than a drunken lout, or the feeling that the army was only sought as an occupation by men who could do no better, there had in fact been considerable investment by the nation in the armed forces, both materially and emotionally. Soldiers (and sailors) had created the Empire and were now its defenders. A quarter of the globe was then governed by the British, and troops were there to make sure that this rule was enforced. Little boys at their desks in school thrilled to stories of derring-do by the men in red coats and later in khaki. So maybe it was one or more of these elements which made David decide that soldiering was for him.

Perhaps his motives were shared by another Glasgow boy named John Cusack, who joined the army just a little earlier. In his book, written as a Chelsea Pensioner, he describes the unrelenting harshness and drudgery of working class life then and the huge impact that seeing soldiers had on him as a youngster. He wrote, 'Often we boys would hear a band, and we'd run to see soldiers marching through the streets', and he admits being stirred by the thrill of it. That feeling remained, and he fed it with reading in the free local public library and by looking at pictures of soldiers. Its crowning moment, he admits, was seeing the Royal Scots Greys on their magnificent mounts one day in the city: 'Those grey horses were the biggest I had ever seen and they set me dreaming of the day when I could run away from home, join the army, and wear a scarlet tunic.' Though 'Scarlet Fever' had well and truly struck him, he never forgot the grimness of his and family's life before joining up and recalled urchins shouting, '"Beef and a tanner a day" – meaning that was the only reason for us having joined the army!'

All of this could have influenced David, but another factor could quite simply have been his age, as the reality was that you had to be in your later teens to join up. The idea of exchanging drudgery and dirt for a spick and span uniform may also have swayed him, but whatever the motive, he came to a decision to leave the council's cleansing department and join the Army, enlisting on 9 February 1914. He signed on for a term of seven years in the ranks with another five in the reserve, thus being eligible to be called up again if his country needed him in a crisis. Many boys joined the forces to get a change of scene, for adventure and to see the world. David could have had no idea just what it would mean for him – and just how soon.

He joined the Cameronians (Scottish Rifles), and its 1st Battalion was based at Maryhill Barracks in 1914, close to home, but its regimental depot was at Hamilton, where new recruits would normally go for six months of basic training. It was hard, aiming to mould soft civilian individuals into soldiers, physically fit and obeying orders immediately and unflinchingly. A man's regiment and the Army were now his home and family, to respect and honour above all. John Lucy, a relatively recent pre-war recruit like David, well recalled the process of becoming a soldier in his famous book *There's a Devil in the Drum*:

> The military vocabulary, minor tactics, knowledge of parts of the rifle, route marches, fatigues, semaphore, judging distance, lectures on *esprit de corps,* and on the history of our regiment, spit and polish, drill, physical training and other, forgotten subjects were rubbed into us for the worst six months of my life . . . In time we effaced ourselves. Our bodies developed and our backs straightened according to plan . . . Pride of arms possessed us, and we discovered that our regiment was a regiment, and then some.

An excellent insight into David's life early in his new career can be provided by the book *Morale – A Study in Men and Courage* by John Baynes. He stresses the qualities of the men thus:

> The Regular soldier of the pre-First World War was not a drunken wastrel fit only to be described as the 'scum of the earth'. There is a picture in many people's minds of the pre-1914 Army as a mass of brutal savages under the control of bored, foppish officers who hardly ever had any contact with them at all. If I can succeed in dispelling any misconceptions about officers I shall be glad, but I shall be happier still to dispose of lingering and ridiculous misjudgements of their soldiers.

Since many of these new recruits would have been working class Glasgow lads from rough backgrounds, a tough environment and hard work would have been nothing new to them. But perhaps stern discipline was. Early starts were the norm, as were seemingly endless inspections, with punishments for the slightest misdemeanour. But there were benefits, too. For some of these men it would be the first time in their lives that they had had three good meals a day and decent clothes. John Cusack wrote that food had been a constant worry in his home and always in short supply when he was young. Little would have been different in the large Cruickshank family. Of equally great importance in the army was cleanliness, which was more than just for the sake of appearance; when men were posted overseas to hot, rugged and far-flung parts of the Empire, their health and very lives could depend on good hygiene.

The military textbook and virtual 'Bible' of this period was the *Infantry Training Manual 1914*, which set the high standards expected of all the soldiers of the nation and empire. It was mandatory reading and had to be mastered, if not exactly word for word by the troops themselves, then certainly by the officers who oversaw and led them. It declared:

> The soldier should be instructed in the deeds which made the British Army and his regiment famous. The privilege which he inherits as a citizen of a great Empire should be explained to him, and he should be taught to appreciate the honour which is his, as a soldier, of serving his King and Country.

The day started at 0600 hrs with Reveille on the bugle, followed by bagpipes. The men received the traditionally strong army mug of tea, known as 'gunfire', on awakening, but it was all downhill after that, with a cold wash and then outside for parade, followed by some tough physical exercise or a run. Breakfast had to be earned, and it was not until after this activity that it would be eaten. Company orders took place at 0900 hrs, when any discipline necessary would be administered but when the men could also see an officer about any problems. Room and kit inspections followed, with everything having to be spotless. Next came training, which fell into three main categories: drill, weapon training, which eventually included shooting, and route marches. These were the solid foundations upon which soldiering stood, and any recruit unable or unwilling to master them was not going to last long. Lunch was at 1200 hrs and then time was given over to sport – games such as football and hockey for team-building as well as fitness, and boxing to foster and channel aggression.

Privacy was minimal at all times, with shared accommodation to promote *esprit de corps* and comradeship. John Cusack found himself sharing his new quarters with thirty-one other recruits. As many of these poor Glasgow lads already came from small and crowded quarters, this perhaps came as no great new shock to them. Bunking in with the recruits, but sometimes with his own area as befitted his status, might be a lance corporal to oversee things. Another meal would be taken in the evening, and the men would turn in to sleep at 2200 hrs, having heard the bugler sound Last Post, and the piper. No doubt a good night's sleep was much needed. Even Sunday was not a day of leisure for the men, with a morning Church Parade and an inspection beforehand to make sure everyone was spick and span; the service itself could well be followed by a march past overseen by a senior officer.

Despite some opinions to the contrary, initiative was sought and nurtured among soldiers. Education was encouraged and there were classes available for those who had left school without sitting exams. Brighter soldiers could go on specialist courses in vital military skills such as signalling or sniping – which also brought the extra bonus of boosting their wages. Promotion and the prospect of rising through the ranks was perhaps not something that troubled David's thoughts too much at this early stage. An able soldier could be appointed lance corporal within a year or two and earn another stripe, making him a corporal, by the end of his service with the Colours; and the promise of being made up to sergeant was often offered as an incentive to make a soldier sign on for a second term. Soldiering could offer a total career, complete with pension, for those who enjoyed and chose to stick with it.

Everything in the Army is done in stages and is (no pun intended!) regimented. Basic training tended to take place early in the year, then soldiers would move into working with higher formations. Once they passed out, there would be some welcome freedom from the barracks, since a recruit could not leave base before then. While the 2nd Battalion was in Malta, David's basic training complete, he joined the 1ˢᵗ Battalion at Maryhill Barracks. It was now the summer of 1914 and things in his little world were ticking along nicely, with not too much to concern him personally. In fact, summer manoeuvres in the Highlands were shortly due which promised to be challenging but also a great adventure.

But in faraway Bosnia and its capital, Sarajevo, events were unfolding which would bring a very different adventure for David and his comrades. If the young soldier had seen the newspapers he might have spotted that Archduke Franz Ferdinand, heir to the throne of the Austro-Hungarian Empire had been assassinated, ironically enough while attending army manoeuvres in a province which the Habsburgs had recently annexed despite warnings about the volatility of the area. The fatal shots fired by a Bosnian Serb student called Gavrilo Princip were to trigger a chain of events which would see Britain involved in its first major war in Europe since Waterloo.

Chapter 2

To War

As the European crisis unravelled, David and his new comrades were training among the Grampian Mountains in northern Perthshire. How much thought he gave to the events so far off or how much information reached the rankers cannot be known, and perhaps in any case there was little energy left for thought after their strenuous days. But some of their officers were certainly well informed, gave the matter some serious thought and did not like the look of things. One of these was Captain James Jack, who noted in his diary on 28 July that tension was now high in Europe following the declaration of war by Austria-Hungary on Serbia. The next day he wrote of newspapers full of the news and of awaiting the outcome.

He did not have to wait long to find out; during a tennis party the next day with fellow officers at Blair Castle, a telegram arrived, and as the most senior officer present he opened it. He recorded:

> We are to return to Glasgow . . . prior to Mobilisation. Tennis ends abruptly; we return to camp; the brigade spends all night packing up beside the patches of pine woods and the splashing waters of the Garry.

The Army had a procedure and it now clicked into place. It did not yet mean war, but war was growing nearer. Within days, Jack had passed through Maryhill and on to a post called Fort Ardhallow near Dunoon on the Clyde, two hours away, with another officer and sixty men, entrenching and wiring. It was here that the young officer got the news he had feared:

> About 2am (5th August) I receive a telegram stating that Britain declared war on Germany at midnight. One can scarcely believe that five Great Powers – also styled 'civilised' – are at

war, and that the original spark . . . arose from the murder of
one man and his wife. It is quite mad as well as being dreadful.

Orders were that mobilization would be completed within four
days, and Jack noted the well-oiled machine in action. As the 'home'
battalion now, his was way under strength and would rely on its some
600 reservists to come back and bring it up to its requisite war
establishment of 1,022; incredibly, only one or two men failed to
show as ordered. Jack was impressed by their condition and wrote,
'Although they require tuning up as soldiers in addition to
conditioning for marching they are splendid fellows. All ranks are in
fine fettle at the prospect of active service.' As someone who had
seen battle in South Africa he said that he personally loathed the
prospect of war. But he did not doubt the cause was just and feared a
future in which 'Prussian war lords dominated'. The subject certainly
dominated the mess, with the hope that their French allies would be
men such as Napoleon led at Ulm, Austerlitz and Jena, rather than
those hammered by these self-same Prussians in 1870/1. Russian
numbers impressed as ever, but there was doubt here too, as the most
recent war involving Russia, against the Japanese, had also resulted
in defeat. Among the enemy, Germany was respected but not feared
by these professional soldiers, and Austria was not too highly
regarded.

In Scotland the war was greeted with the same broad enthusiasm
seizing the rest of Europe, and many saw a particular reason why a
small country should stand and fight. The *Scotsman* newspaper
warned that Belgium's fate could be Scotland's:

> In time, and probably no long time, it would be our turn to fall
> victims to the greed and ambition of a Power which, to judge
> by the latest development in its policy, is prepared to go to any
> lengths of force and cunning to attain its ends and that regards
> no rights as sacred except its own.

But the newspaper also carried a report of an anti-war
demonstration in Edinburgh, albeit one broken up by a larger crowd.
Then on 10 August a rally of 5,000 anti-war protesters met in
Glasgow. Local reporters recorded that when James McDougall, a

well-known socialist sacked by his employer for his political activities, told the crowd that the war was a needless capitalist jaunt which would aid only profiteers and harm workers, he was cheered. However, most of the cheering was for the war.

As professionals, David and his comrades readied themselves to be among the first involved. Captain Jack was told by an ex-Staff College friend that the German infantry was equal to ours, although we handled our rifles better, while our artillery and cavalry should prove superior. Jack joked with his friend Sam Darling on departure that his rolled kit looked like a corpse, only to be met not with the expected smile or witty retort but a hard stare and the reply: 'If we ever get into a European war few of us will ever see the end of it.' There was in fact a wider recognition that the war might be long and require many recruits. An appeal was issued by Kitchener, the new Minister of War:

> I feel certain that Scotsmen have only to know that the country urgently needs their services to offer them with the same splendid patriotism as they have always shown in the past. Tell them from me that their services were never more needed than they are today and that I rely confidently on a splendid response to the national appeal.

He was not disappointed, and in David's city 20,000 men passed through the Gallowgate recruiting office alone, according to the *Glasgow Herald* newspaper.

Meanwhile, spy scares abounded throughout the country as the regulars were prepared for departure to the front. Captain Jack noted that secret orders arrived for leaving on 13 August. He wrote:

> The battalion carries out its usual programme to avoid advertising the move to the public, among whom there are certain to be foreign spies. After the day's exercises are finished the pipes and drums play us back to barracks through thronged streets; but there is no fuss, just the friendly wave of hands. The four companies, each 220 strong and wearing full equipment, look splendid as they swing in at the barrack gate for the last time.

Were David's loved ones, who lived so close, among the crowd watching their soldier boy marching off to war?

That night, between 2300 hrs and 0100 hrs of the following morning, the battalion unobtrusively slipped away from Maryhill station on four special trains with 'a few loiterers (to) give us a cheer and wish us good luck'. It would be almost five years before David saw his home city again. By the afternoon they were at Southampton on the English south coast, almost 400 miles away, waiting for darkness to cover their crossing of the Channel to what they hoped and believed would be France – and indeed proved to be Le Havre. It was a dull day as dawn broke, but nothing could dent their spirits as they saw the huge cheering French crowds intent on giving them a rousing reception.

Almost everyone on both sides predicted a short and victorious war, the British by Christmas and the Germans before the autumn leaves fell. David would have shared this confidence. Instilled into all British soldiers from the very moment they joined up was the belief that they were the best in the world. Moreover, they were supported by the mighty Royal Navy ruling the Seven Seas, and if this was not enough, there was the fact that a quarter of the globe was shaded imperial red and the position was simple: when Britain was at war, her Empire was at war too. The view was that the Germans were upstarts soon to be put back into their place – an operation as sweet as it would be swift.

For some years before 1914 a delicate alliance system had meant, theoretically, that war was impossible due to a 'balance of power'. At Europe's centre were Germany and Austria-Hungary, natural bedfellows. Balancing them was the more recent pairing of France and Russia. Others players would have major parts in that summer drama – chiefly Serbia and Britain. Serbia was blamed for Franz Ferdinand's death as Princip, his assassin, was a Serb nationalist (though actually Bosnian and an Austrian citizen). And Britain, as the world's most powerful nation, was unlikely to stay aloof.

To win the war quickly, Germany had her Schlieffen Plan, aiming to overcome the problem of fighting both France and Russia by sending her Austro-Hungarian allies east while the French were smashed by an overwhelming westward German thrust. Taking Paris within weeks would force a French surrender, then attention would turn east again while the unwieldy Russians were still gearing up. France's eyes were fixed foremost on her territory lost to Germany in 1871. Much effort and money had gone into modernizing her military, and their thinking now favoured the 'cult of the offensive'; any potential leader who thought otherwise was largely ridiculed and sidelined.

While Britain might have seemed aloof from Europe, she had not obtained the world's largest empire by ignoring world events, and imperial interests had periodically brought clashes with the other Great Powers. For many years the major antagonists had been the French, but they had drawn closer in the first decade of the twentieth century. The same went for Russia. Put simply, Britain could not tolerate any threat to her sea lanes – especially those closest to home. The half-British Kaiser Wilhelm, the grandson of Queen Victoria and a previous visitor to Cowes Regatta, should have known this, but he had a strange love-hate relationship with the nation of his maternal forebears. 'Kaiser Bill' was mocked by the British press and public, but all he wanted was for his country to be more like Britain, with an imperial 'place in the sun' and a large navy to go with it. He misunderstood the British psyche, and failed to see where his competitiveness or sabre-rattling might lead.

In the month-long crisis after the Archduke's assassination, secret military and governmental talks about how a British force would embark for France to meet any German threat no longer seemed fanciful. The British hoped not to fight any future war in Britain, and the Royal Navy and the trickiness of an invasion made a German one unlikely. Britain's view was that it would better to fight on foreign soil and support the French if they were invaded, before halting the Germans and then defeating them. Popular distrust of the French would not stop a military alliance, but the plans for one were never made public. However, Britain's army was tiny compared to the vast conscripted forces of the major European powers. Indeed, the Germans would soon sneer at Britain's 'contemptible little army', which, they said, would be of little use against their might; there was also a rare example of German humour when they promised they would send the Berlin police force along to arrest it.

By German standards it may have been a good joke, but their laughter would be short-lived, for though small, the British Army had certain advantages. Its troops were well trained, well led, highly motivated and considered themselves second to none. And the 'old sweats' among these regulars knew things, some of them hard-gained at the hands of the Boers, such as the importance of rifle fire. As a result, every infantryman could fire at least fifteen aimed rounds a minute. This would be a major factor in the early tussles.

Although secret plans laid the groundwork for the movement, arrival and dispersal of British forces coming to France, there was still a problem. Due to the two-battalion system, one on active service abroad and the other at home, only the overseas battalion was ever at full strength and was often far away. The home battalion contained new recruits and provided a feeder system for the unit abroad, while time-expired soldiers passed into the reserves, meaning that there was very little experience in the home unit. On mobilization, reservists were ordered to rejoin and could make up some 60 per cent of the 1,000-strong battalion.

David fitted perfectly the picture of a home battalion recruit and had just completed his training. While serving soldiers were physically fit, the same could not always be said of reservists, some of whom had been civilians for several years now, more portly perhaps and with softer feet in the absence of army boots and marching. But, as Captain Jack's diary noted, the timetable and overall plan went smoothly, and his men were in France on 15 August – just eleven days after Britain's entry into war. The 'Cams' were now on active service, and as such an officer recorded their daily doings in the form of the battalion's war diary.

Le Havre may indeed have looked suitably 'foreign' to David and his comrades, but there were strong ties between the Scots and the French (often united in the past against the English!) and they were treated like conquering heroes before they had even seen the Germans. The sights and smells were all different and exciting but there was no mistaking the warmth of this Gallic welcome. Communication was often a problem, but very welcome and clearly understood were the many offers of wine or brandy and the requests for souvenirs such as buttons or cap badges.

While this was all fun and may have eased the pangs of homesickness perhaps already niggling some of the younger soldiers like David, it was not going to stop the Germans and win the war.

And so it was soon down to what the infantry does best – marching. In this case it was a theoretically easy 5 miles from Le Havre to a camp where some sorting out was done. For the returning reservists it was a mere taste of what they were letting themselves in for – welcome back to the army – and no doubt their feet told the tale afterwards!

The Cams spent only one day in their new French abode and at 0530 hrs on 17 August they were all loaded onto a train which clanked and chugged forward for the next fourteen hours. These trains soon became infamous to the British. While for the officers there might at least be some resemblance to travel back home, in normal carriages with seats, for the other ranks there were cattle trucks marked 'Chevaux [horses] 8 Hommes [men] 40', which was soon understood to mean forty of them as the passengers. If they were lucky there was sometimes a layer of straw.

But excitement was still high and the men were keen to get at the Germans, so they endured their transport as a means to an end. At least it was surely better than walking – though this may have been questioned later, as the train crawled along, sometimes so slowly that they could get off and walk alongside. And there were many stops – handy at first for a leg stretch and a smoke, but soon irritating and frustrating. No information came about the delays, so there was little else to do but grouse and conjecture – something which Tommy did with aplomb.

They were heading east and their journey, despite its duration, was only 175 miles to Busigny, from where three of the four companies marched to billets at Maretz two miles away, near the Belgian border. But before that the locals had welcomed them, the entire village turning out for a civic reception. They were all reunited in the morning and for the next two days the whole battalion unloaded the train and sorted kit. This done, on 21 August, A Company marched to Valenciennes, 25 miles away, where they were joined the next day by the rest of the battalion and formed headquarters. The war had not seemed real up to this point, but things were soon to change.

Despite the confidence of the British, they were on the back foot in the fledgling war; and while there might be talk of advancing towards Berlin, it was the Germans who called the early shots. A massive German force was swinging through Belgium, as set out in the Schlieffen Plan, to sweep around and encircle Paris. It was known that the Germans were heading this way and that there would be a clash, but confidence was high. A reality check was soon to come, however, as the Commander-in-Chief, Sir John French, initially had no idea of the size of his enemy. When reality dawned, and certainly when the fighting began, it became clear that what the British Army would soon be engaging in was a struggle to prevent itself being overwhelmed. A defensive line was chosen on the Mons-Condé canal, with a fall-back position a couple of miles behind if needed. It was not perfect but had to suffice, a line 20 miles long with troops thinly stretched along it.

Even as the opening shots of the Battle of Mons were being fired, the urgency of the situation was being felt by the Cams. At 0800 hrs they were marched six miles to an outpost line at Vicq to await further orders. These soon came as things at Mons started to unravel, and at 1300 hrs they travelled another three miles to Condé and the canal, where with the Middlesex to their right they were forming the extreme left wing of the British position. The seriousness of the situation was made clear to them: they were to hold their position at all costs.

Communications were poor in 1914, and actually neither side knew their enemy's exact position. The French were giving ground and the British were in blissful ignorance that their flank was open – and being made more so by advancing. This was also the German view; despite being in contact with the French for some time now and advancing, they did not believe the British were close. British cavalry in a skirmish near Mons on 22 August had been taken for scouts. German tactics bear this out, as they initially attacked in massed, solid formation, confident that their seemingly unstoppable progress would continue. They were soon disabused of this idea.

Their ignorance was shared by the folk of Mons and surrounding villages. On Sunday, 23 August people were out and about in their Sunday best, many going to church, as the first shots were exchanged. Of crucial importance were the canal crossings, for if the Germans were to advance, they had to use them. Although the Germans foolishly tried to swamp the British positions early on, with little gain, they quickly learned their lesson and soon brought artillery up to support their attacks; now the British infantry suffered. And such were the Germans' numbers that it was only a matter of time before they broke through.

Due to the echeloned German swing through Belgium they did not all come into action at the same time; thus the defenders west of Mons got some respite along the canal, but when the attack inevitably came they put up the same determined resistance. It was during this crisis period that 19 Brigade, to which the Cams belonged, was ordered forward at great haste.

It was not only the right flank of the British Army which was in peril. There was danger on the left too, with only a weak French territorial division out there somewhere and some cavalry. It was not a reassuring position. As the Cams reached the canal, the first men of General von Kluck's First Army were arriving. Von Kluck, whose name almost inevitably, given British military humour, featured in a rude marching song, was completely surprised, believing no enemy within 50 miles of his front.

The surprise was mutual, but word of the accurate and sustained firepower of the British had perhaps got around, for as the Cams took up their hastily sketched line, the Germans seemed reluctant and their attacks half-hearted; they certainly came off worse in these clashes. The 1st Battalion, the Middlesex Regiment, to the right of the Cams, were having a harder time, but holding. Records show that only one Cameronian died on 23 August, Lance Corporal George Young, but there would also, inevitably, have been men wounded. All in all, they were pretty satisfied with their action and sure that they could hold on. But the wider picture was not so rosy, for the Germans were through in several places further along and their position would only become stronger as more troops got across. And the longer the British tarried the more isolated they would become, since it became clear that the French were still pulling back. It was time to cut and run.

The defence along the canal had been stalwart and the German hope of rapidly sweeping the British aside was dashed. A major part had been played by sheer British tenacity, repeatedly holding off overwhelmingly superior numbers, chiefly with rifle fire. All 1914 riflemen could fire fifteen aimed rounds a minute – many considerably more – from their Short Magazine Lee Enfields, and the enemy in some places believed massed machine guns were holding them off; in fact, the British had just two machine guns per battalion, as did the Germans.

The Germans' day had been one of surprise and frustration – surprise at even finding the British in their way, and then frustration at their tenacity, only retreating when no other course was open and making the Germans pay dearly for any advance. Frustration also came in the lack of a positive breakthrough, for it was considered by most that the British would be swept aside easily. This is reflected in the account of a German regimental officer, Captain Walter Bloem, who admitted in a book published in 1916 that his men had openly mocked the British before the battle. He recorded of that evening:

> The men were all chilled to the bone, almost too exhausted to move and with the depressing consciousness of defeat weighing upon them. A bad defeat, there could be no gainsaying it; in our first battle we had been badly beaten, and by the English – by the English that we had laughed at a few hours before.

They had learned a hard lesson and were not laughing at them now.

The British perhaps felt two main emotions after Mons. They had planned to hold the Germans and there was the satisfaction of having done so; despite being outnumbered and outgunned, they had certainly not been outfought. But when the orders came through to fall back, Tommy could not understand it. Having stopped the Germans, where was the order to advance and push them back? But as ever, orders were not there to be questioned but simply obeyed.

By later standards, Mons was small fry. The British lost some 1,600 men killed, wounded and captured. The Germans' losses of around 5,000 shocked them hugely. But the importance of Mons cannot be overstated. The massive, confident German army had been stopped in its tracks at its first encounter with the derided British. If there was perhaps another emotion for the Germans it was anger at this fact, something they aimed soon to reverse. Mons would not end the war. Indeed, the Allies were still in big trouble. But the British had not been crushed, France had not suffered the demoralizing blow of losing her ally, and both nations would fight on.

Chapter 3

Le Cateau

Ahead for the British was something actually harder than standing and fighting. It was the task of disengaging from an enemy at near full throttle and still aiming to crush them with a much bigger force. German momentum may have stalled but almost certainly had not been stopped completely. However, tight corners were nothing new to the British Army; arguably, some of its finest moments had come in such circumstances and it was about to prove again that a backs-to-the-wall position did not mean defeat.

For David and his mates it meant that they had almost no sooner got into position and started to exchange fire with the enemy than they were ordered to pull back again, at 1400 hrs. Bear in mind that these men had already done much marching by now, faced the strain of battle and were lacking sleep. Their initial movement saw them travel half a mile along the enemy positions, facing dangerous enfilade fire, before retiring a mile to the rear. They could hear the din of battle further away to their left as the Germans stirred, perhaps in pursuit. But their discipline and skill saw them safely cover a 14-mile withdrawal to reach their destination at Jenlain, where they were praised by the Brigade Staff.

British High Command was now aware of its difficulty. Although a good fight was being talked up by some, there was really only one course of action open: to continue retiring in the best order possible in the circumstances, in the hope that they would live to fight another day. David's unit was part of General Horace Smith-Dorrien's II Corps, which had been involved in most of the fighting at Mons. But there was also General Douglas Haig's I Corps, and key to any withdrawal was to try to maintain a unified opposition to the threat bearing down on them. For the Cams this meant one rest day at Jenlain before marching 15 miles to Haussy, the war diary recording the men now 'turning very foot sore and tired'.

The British were at least retreating on their lines of

communication and supply which should have made things easier, especially with rations, but in reality there was great confusion, and a problem soon arose which would affect David directly: tired and dazed men got separated from their units and became stragglers. All were now exhausted and some fell asleep on the march, having to be kicked awake after their short rest periods. Tired soldiers also hallucinated. This aspect was seized on by journalists desperate to report something positive, and so was born the legend of the Angel of Mons intervening to save the Tommies. It was twaddle, but brought some comfort at the time.

Now, too, the British drew the geographical short straw, for along the line of their united retreat was the 20,000-acre Forest of Mormal, and the two corps were forced to separate around it – not a happy proposition. The dense wood had few linking roads, so if either corps was attacked there would be no chance of receiving help. Hopefully, they would be able to reunite and retire to a defensible position on the line of the towns of Le Cateau and Cambrai. Tension was high and matters were made worse by these same roads being choked with fleeing refugees and their belongings.

Le Cateau was now British HQ, and as Smith-Dorrien's staff arrived in the late afternoon of 25 August there was little to cheer them. Haig's corps was eight miles away and the men of II Corps had become horribly mixed and were still coming in after midnight. Their corps commander knew that after three days of fighting and marching they could not now take much more. They would turn and fight if ordered, but they sorely needed a lift. As Smith-Dorrien settled his own HQ at Bertry nearby, orders came to continue retiring the next day. He consulted his divisional commanders, who confirmed what he already knew. His cavalry added that their dispersal meant they could not hold the line of retreat for the infantry by dawn. The best policy, it was suggested, would be to slip away beforehand and forestall the inevitable German attack.

But Smith-Dorrien had another idea. Perhaps it would be best not to break and run, thereby risking further confusion, lack of cohesion, fatigue and hunger and giving the Germans the opportunity to make easy meat of them. Why not stand at Le Cateau and deal the Germans a bloody nose, thus allowing the British to get away under better conditions? Of course he would need the permission of BEF

Commander-in-Chief, Sir John French, which he sought. French was worried and his response was non-committal, but this was good enough for Smith-Dorrien. He would stand and fight.

Some sense of the speed of events now comes from Captain Jack, who was ordered to Le Cateau for orders and to seek billets for the men. He found it full of troops, transports and locals. All seemed in good spirits, which surprised him given the enemy's proximity. This mood was shared at GHQ, where he found the staff operating at full tilt. On reporting to a smart young staff officer he was told that 19 Brigade would billet in the town that night and that orders were being prepared. Jack eyed the cakes and teacups on a table and the staff officer, spotting his bedraggled state, kindly told him to go and get a meal and report back in an hour. Jack happily went off to stuff himself with an omelette, bread and butter and coffee. However, a very different scene greeted his return; everyone had disappeared without trace.

Jack also noted the local population starting to move out, prompted undoubtedly by the sound of the German guns and some shelling of the town itself. As billets he chose some buildings near the railway marshalling yard, not central but crucially on the opposite side to the enemy, with the extra advantage that retreat from there would be easier if needed, as seemed likely, he noted. It took four hours for the brigade to stagger in, the last at 2300 hrs, but there was a hot meal and the promise of a little rest, for dawn would bring another hard day.

There was little time to prepare for battle. Indeed, some units only got their orders at 0500 hrs, an hour before the Germans attacked. The British 'front' as it stood was about 10 miles long, with fire scrapes for infantry cover. But it was perfect for gunners, ideal for defensive artillery, open and with good direct lines of fire. If the Germans had learned at Mons to respect the British rifleman, they were about to get a repeat performance at Le Cateau, this time from the gunners. The Germans tried a pincer movement, because one lesson they had learned from those riflemen at Mons was the need to try and blast them into submission before sending their own men in.

It was around 0600 hrs that the first concentrated shelling started to hit the line, with an instant reply from the British guns. The Germans hoped to pin down their enemy's centre, turning the flanks.

It was a fair idea as the British left was tentatively held by stretched French cavalry and the right was open, with a gap to I Corps which some British battalions filled piecemeal. It was to try and bolster the position to the right that the Cams were first ordered at 0600 hrs, in pursuance of their earlier role of filling in where and when most needed.

Le Cateau saw incredibly steadfast defending by the British Army, and despite constant German blows the old sweats and newer men like David held them off for several hours. Details are unnecessary here, but suffice it to say that Le Cateau arguably saved the BEF from destruction and prevented a complete German victory in the west. As such, it was debatably more important than Mons but it has become an almost 'forgotten battle'. By early afternoon the British knew it was time to go – if this could now be achieved. Le Cateau had served its purpose and the casualty figures showed that it had been much bloodier than Mons, with just under 8,000 British losses. German estimates varied between 15,000 and 30,000.

A crucial document for historians is the war diary. Depending on the dedication, skill or interest of the officer keeping them, these can be illuminating or frustrating. They log locations, movements, actions and casualties and sometimes give a real taste of battle. Sadly, the Cams' diary is hugely disappointing as the original was thrown away on retiring from Le Cateau. Exhausted soldiers – and clearly officers too – disposed of everything deemed not vital to survival. This was later greeted with fury by the commanding officer, and the offender was hauled over the coals and fined. The diary was recreated from memory but is inevitably terse and lacks detail.

The abbreviated diary thus covers the whole battle for the unit in only nine lines, noting the order to the front at 0600 hrs, the taking up of the left of this position four hours later, and the receipt of orders to withdraw to Montigny, 2½ miles behind the front, at 1430 hrs and then to Bertry ninety minutes later. From here the battalion acted as rearguard in a more general move to Maretz, another 2½ miles away. The final remark for that momentous day notes that at 2130 hrs an all-night march to St Quentin began – thankfully, due to the heroics at Le Cateau, without enemy pursuit. For the moment, the British had gained the desired effect from their stand and taken the wind out of the Germans' sails. Whether a roll call was taken that day is unknown

– probably not in the circumstances, though one may have been recorded in the original draft – but no casualty figures are listed.

Another reason for this could be that the unit took no casualties. The CD *Soldiers Who Died in the Great War* lists no 1st Cams killed on 26 August 1914. But it is unlikely that there were none wounded in such a battle or that no men were simply lost in the confusion. The *Official History of the Great War* gives no breakdown of battalion losses but lists those for 19 Brigade as 477 men at Le Cateau. Divided between the four battalions making up the brigade, this it would put the losses of each at nearly 120 men wounded, taken prisoner and missing. The *OH* stresses these figures do not include missing men later returning to duty, but sadly does not number these. The battalion's own war diary later lists 300 such men, almost a third of the unit. One of them was David Cruickshank.

Chapter 4

Going Missing

Escaping from Le Cateau, but later captured for a short time, was a senior officer of the Cams whose family would later play an important role in David's story. Major Crofton Bury Vandeleur, aged forty-seven, and David Cruickshank came from worlds apart. Vandeleur had been born into the Army in India and a military career had always beckoned. His and David's paths crossed briefly in 1914, but later in the war, at perhaps David's lowest ebb, the Vandeleurs would play a massive part in his life.

There are many discrepancies in the two existing versions of events surrounding David's first meeting with his saviour, Julie-Celestine Baudhuin. They were given some years after the event and both will be recounted here. It would have been a situation of stress and confusion for both parties, and memory is not always the most reliable of recording devices.

The war diary has the battalion coming under German shrapnel fire the day before the battle. Was David injured then, since he mentions a wound when in Le Cateau the next day? While the men were ordered off at 0600 hrs from the goods yard on 26 August, David's account suggests he was still in the town at around 0900 hrs. Again, the war diary perhaps gives some clue, as the next orders listed come at 1000 hrs, much nearer David's estimate. Were they all still in town, or only some of them, as they moved off? Perhaps the mistake is in the reconstituted diary?

Mme Baudhuin was thirty-eight and a mother of three living in a small house in Le Cateau on Rue de Pont Bleu when David came into her already troubled life. Her husband Jules, three years her senior, and their son of the same name aged twenty were at the front. Jules junior was soon to go missing in action and his father captured. She was now caring alone for Léon, seventeen, and Marie, twelve. She later said that David's proximity in age to her own soldier son and the anxiety she knew his mother would be going through very much guided her when she discovered the bewildered and frightened young man.

David said he was with a soldier called Private Parker on the street at 0900 hrs on 26 August when they ran into Germans who opened fire, and they became separated. As he ran he saw more Germans blocking his escape route and they too fired. He fell, playing dead, and it seemed to have worked as the enemy moved off. He was terrified, with little experience other than his six months in the Army which could not have prepared him for this.

Madame Baudhuin recalled David running to her door on seeing her looking out into the street and waving his arms about wildly, shouting 'Moi tué' [me dead] and 'Maman soleil' [Mother sunshine]. She said:

> He was in a sorry state and almost mad. At the time I didn't know which saint to trust in, but the decision to bring him into the house and hide him at all costs was quickly made. I thought of the mother of the agitated young man. We gave this poor escapee something to eat and fixed him up a hiding place in a shed at the bottom of the little garden at the back of the house.

The Baudhuins spoke no English but David clearly had some French, for being asked by Léon if he was 'Anglais' he replied 'Ecossais' [Scottish].

David continued:

> One of the bullets wounded me slightly, but most of them went into the wall of the *estaminet* [a pub – a later request to dig them out as souvenirs was refused by the owner]. Almost blinded by the dust from the splintered wall, I zigzagged along the middle of the street which was strewn with the bodies of men and horses.

It was then he decided to play dead.

> To my immense relief and surprise the two parties of Germans moved off in opposite directions. I had been the only living

object seen by them in the street and they must have felt satisfied that I was riddled with bullets.

His comrade Parker now slipped his mind, and there is no one of that name recorded as dying at Le Cateau. This is not the only inconsistency in his story, as David was later to recall seeing a second figure – another woman:

During the battle in the streets of Le Cateau I was on her doorstep riposting to the attack of several Germans when she arrived carrying a bucket of water. A bullet meant for me went through the bucket, while another made a hole in her clothes and skimmed her leg. Standing in the doorstep holding her pierced bucket, she must have studied my face carefully and thus my appearance became graved in her memory.

This fleeting encounter with Madame D, as David called her, was to have grave consequences for both of them. The biggest difference in the stories comes from David again:

For a while I lay among the dead on the road; then, being convinced that the enemy was really gone, I went through a narrow passage that led into the gardens at the back of the houses. At the time the gardens were in full growth, and I lay down for about an hour in the shelter of the hedges and flowers. In that position, where I seemed to be the only creature about, I gathered a general idea of the fighting that was going on. From the high road surrounding the town our artillery was trying to drive the Germans out. The enemy was, however, in possession of the town in very strong force, and was not to be dislodged. Loss of blood from my new wound and one I had received the previous day made me feel faint, so I crept on all-fours along the garden up to the nearest house. I saw the cellar door was open and crawled in. The sight of beer and wine on the table was a sensation to me in my exhausted and famished condition. I was helping myself to a glass of white wine, when I heard footsteps on the cellar stairs. I still had my rifle. I levelled it at the forthcoming shadow. Fortunately, I realized that it must be that of a woman . . . Often in later days I felt a shiver run through me on reflecting how near I had been to mistaking this splendid woman for a pursuing German. She took pity on me instantly and, with very few words, helped me to food and drink.

So why these differences? It is hard to be certain. In telling his story to a journalist many years later did David try to make it more exciting? His 'riposting of several Germans' smacks of this. Surely Madame Baudhuin would have recalled a rifle pointed at her in her own house, though David did not say it was still trained on her when she entered the cellar? Why does she have the initial encounter taking place at her door? Why is a table with drink on it in the cellar? It is possible that the family had fled down there for safety because of the shelling.

There are some intriguing bits of potentially supporting evidence which back David's version. A Private Walter Parker did serve, and if he was present he survived to rejoin his unit, for sadly he died in November. David mentions escaping down a narrow passage into rear gardens. Rue de Pont Bleu was later renamed Rue Carlier but it is pretty much unchanged. Only three houses, all joined in the terrace, were destroyed in later shelling, but sadly one of these was the Baudhuin residence. They were not rebuilt, but the gap was filled with three garages, each having the same frontage as the cottages and still bearing their house numbers. And between two of them there is still a small passageway from the street to the gardens – perhaps a communal right of access meant that it had to be left, but there it most certainly still is. And the enigmatic Madame D would certainly appear again.

Whatever the details, David's plight immediately moved Madame Baudhuin, who later said:

Ah, how he was young and little. It struck me that he had almost lost his reason. He muttered unconnected words in French. But frequently he repeated, 'Allemands, non, non' [Germans, no, no], making it clear that he dreaded being taken prisoner by the Germans. What touched me more than anything else, however, was his repetition in the wanderings of his mind, of the word 'maman' and it brought to my mind more strongly than ever thoughts of my boy Jules, who might at that very moment be in a similar plight.

David could not have known it at the time, nor have totally understood what it was all going to mean for him and these kind French folk, but his active service of just eleven days had come to an end. His war, however, was far from over, and danger was going to be perhaps even more ever-present for him than for his comrades who had marched from Le Cateau to continue fighting.

Chapter 5

In Hiding

The Baudhuin family, or Julie-Celestine as its de facto head, now had a big decision to make about what to do with this stranded and wounded British soldier. He was frightened, alone and, crucially, a boy of a similar age to her own cherished firstborn, now also in uniform and in danger from the common enemy. It did not take too long for Julie-Celestine to realize that there was only one decision she could make – and that was to keep this boy safe from the Germans. Perhaps in time circumstances would allow him to rejoin his own kind, as the enemy might be repulsed speedily or David might be able to get away. In reaching this decision, as much with her heart as with her head, Julie-Celestine was perhaps not initially aware of the potential danger it involved.

David could obviously not be kept in open view and so a *cachette* (hiding place) was quickly made for him. While he lay concealed there Julie-Celestine began to realize that this young Cameronian could be the source of great danger to her and her children. The Germans, who had pushed the British and French armies further south during the past few days, were now occupying the town in strength and beginning to take control of the civilian population. Many German soldiers were being billeted in the houses of the townsfolk and patrols could and did arrive unannounced at any hour to search for contraband or to requisition a variety of items from householders who had little enough to begin with.

German control was quickly established with the formation of *Kommandanturen* (command offices) in the towns or larger villages which were set up mostly in town halls or civic buildings. Le Cateau was chosen as it was already the natural centre for the local area. Each *Kommandantur* was headed by a senior military officer, assisted by an inspecting and land officer who quickly got to work surveying what an occupied area could provide to support the invaders. The office staff might only be small, perhaps six or eight, but they were backed by men from the military police – soon to be dubbed by the local population *les diables verts* (the green devils) due to their uniforms. Regular soldiers, often recovering wounded men not yet fit again for the front line, were frequently used to patrol the town's roads and carry out checks, with elder reservists often posted throughout the countryside.

In time, civilian bureaucrats were sometimes also brought in from Germany to oversee the maintenance of this system and they often brought their pettifogging ways with them. Alongside the newly imposed German authorities, the conquerors also let the pre-war French local civil powers carry out some roles which were useful to them in maintaining control and cohesion. Towns and villages were allowed to keep their mayors, but often the existing office-holder was taken into custody, to show the new bosses meant business, and replaced by his deputy. This was certainly the case in Le Cateau. Thus the familiar French gendarmes were still to be seen on the streets and it was expected that they would maintain the rule of law – as imposed by their new masters. New edicts appeared through proclamations and they were soon coming thick and fast. The effective head of Le Cateau was Major Haertel, whose name soon became a familiar sight at the bottom of notices. Some locals claimed he had inside knowledge of the town, having worked there a dozen or so years before the war, and that this was how he got the job. Another unverified rumour was that he was the son of a German general.

The Germans knew that there were cut off British troops at large in and around the town as some had been caught within days of Le Cateau's fall. This also caused the Germans to suspect that there were many others who had gone to ground. The dense woods in the area offered ideal cover for soldiers on the run and the late August weather had been warm, making it reasonably comfortable to live outdoors; these men after all were trained soldiers and not afraid of roughing it, although most were in a far from ideal condition, exhausted or suffering from wounds. Men such as these were likely to pose a great problem to the occupying forces. They were regular soldiers or reservists, who knew how to use the arms they carried and could be dangerous. German troops had been made well aware of the potential problem of so-called *franc tireurs* – the partisans from the Franco-Prussian War who had picked off occupying soldiers individually or carried out acts of sabotage. There was no way such a development was going to be allowed in this conflict.

The 1914–18 archive in Le Cateau contains many personal accounts of events in the town during the occupation. One is from André Moguet, born in 1908 – although he was only six years old at the time, the period held vivid and often disturbing memories for him. This was most harshly illustrated as early as November 1914 by the warnings issued to the civilian population about ignoring or disobeying the rules laid down by the occupiers. Moguet recalled how two local men, Alfred Lallier and M L'Homme, were found in possession of pigeons, something which was strictly against orders as it was feared they could be used to send messages to the Allies. The reality was that pigeons were often kept in the countryside as a cheap additional source of food. But the Germans were not interested in the reality. It was important that they prove a point. The two men were immediately arrested and charged, then given a brief trial at which they were allowed no legal representation; they were found guilty and sentenced to be shot by firing squad, a sentence duly carried out at the edge of a wood on the outskirts of town.

Julie-Celestine must have been fully aware that she and her family were now in the greatest of danger, since the Germans were convinced that there were British soldiers still at large in the area. Proclamations had been posted throughout the region warning the local population against foolishly providing any assistance to enemy soldiers on the run and making it clear that the penalties for any such action would be swift and severe. Further proclamations advised all soldiers at large that if they gave themselves up they would be treated as prisoners of war, but that those who did not would be treated as spies and executed when caught.

The fewer people who knew about the presence of the fugitive in the Baudhuin home the better it would be. However, Julie-Celestine also knew that this young Scot needed treatment for his wounds as well as for his exhausted condition. For over a week he had lain there in a state of semi-consciousness. In desperation, she took into her confidence a local medical man, Dr Pierre Tison, who with a trained nurse, Mlle Madeleine Mutin, treated David. With the constant care of Julie-Celestine, he began to recover, and after a further week of rest his strength slowly returned. To begin with, David had been content to remain in the loft of the tiny house and spent much of his time asleep. As his health and strength improved he began to spend more and more time with the family in their living quarters, consisting of a few rooms, none of which could be considered spacious. This, too, was not without dangers.

David was quickly becoming a member of the Baudhuin family. In a 1921 interview Julie-Celestine said she was tortured by an ominous lack of news from the front about her husband and son and she lavished her motherly attention on David, while her younger children Léon and Marie came to think of him as a brother. He was rapidly developing his knowledge of the local French patois, so initial communication difficulties were soon being overcome. He was also becoming more confident in his homely surroundings, a confidence which proved eventually to play a part in his downfall. Spending most of his time in the family rooms and away from his *cachette* presented an additional problem for Julie-Celestine, for the Germans would often arrive suddenly at houses in the town to conduct searches or to requisition food or household goods. Mercifully, they did not visit the house during the period when David was most seriously ill, but the tension for the family would have been unbearable, knowing the consequences if David was discovered.

The occupiers were settling in and taking control, and German soldiers were billeted in many buildings in the town, often in the homes of townspeople. Fortunately, the Baudhuin house had not been selected as a billet. As far as the Germans were concerned, anything in the town could be requisitioned or used for their purposes. As time went on, they imposed strict rationing on the population, and if anything over and above these rations was found it would be removed and the offender fined or imprisoned for a period.

On one occasion David was downstairs with Julie-Celestine and the children when the Germans began hammering on the door. He bolted upstairs and climbed into the loft. This space was M-shaped, with a flat area about two feet wide between the sloping roofs. There were no dividing walls between the lofts of the adjoining houses – three properties in one direction and five in the other. Quickly and as quietly as he could, David scrambled across the beams and lowered himself into the house three doors away. By now some very close friends and neighbours had been let into the secret, so it was no great surprise for this householder to see David rush downstairs and make for the cellar at the back of the house. David threw himself down the cellar steps and into the darkest corner, away from the tiny air vent which gave a chink of daylight. Crouching there he cowered, his heart pounding from exertion and fear, terrified that the Germans might burst in and arrest him.

Back in the Baudhuin home, reluctant hostess Julie-Celestine served the Germans a glass of wine, more in the hope of gaining a few precious minutes than out of genuine hospitality, and for a few moments they talked, the men questioning her about any extra food she might have secreted away. She laughed heartily at the idea of there being any surplus supplies in her house; it was difficult enough to acquire sufficient for her family. At this time, in October 1914, the Germans were taking the strictest measures to unearth any hidden goods. First the civic authority at the local town hall had been ordered to make out a list of existing stocks in the town; now the German soldiers were carrying out searches to ensure that nothing beyond ration allowances was being held back. The inhabitants were warned by proclamation that the severest penalties would be inflicted on the acting mayor himself or on any individual who was concealing stocks that ought to have been declared. But the question of food stores did not worry Julie-Celestine, for the discovery of David would bring disaster to her and her family.

Despite her denials, the Germans searched each room, opening the doors of every cupboard and checking for contraband. Every nook and cranny was inspected, but it looked as though this visit was going to pass off without incident until they spotted the loft access. A 1937 article in *Chambers Journal* reported it thus:

The Germans decided that their duty compelled them to search the grenier. Madame watched in horror as they ascended the stairs not knowing that David was by now concealed in a neighbouring cellar. One of the soldiers pulled aside few boxes and gave an excited shout. He had come across the bedding on which the young Scot slept.

'What is the meaning of this? Who sleeps here?'

This was a serious matter. 'Léon sleeps here sometimes', the woman answered.

'And he piles up these boxes to hide his bed? A likely story! You are deceiving us, Madame.'

'The boy has curious fads,' she replied. 'He has his own bed downstairs, but he likes to sleep here sometimes. Besides, I am hoping that my soldier son, Jules, will come home on leave and I am keeping an extra bed ready for him. But, I'm afraid there is little chance of my boy or his father getting leave. I should be satisfied to know that they are well – that they are alive indeed.'

Tears came to her eyes, she was a brave French wife and mother, and they were Germans, Boches as they were called.

'This story of the bed is suspicious, Mother,' one of the Germans said. 'Be careful'.

The warning was given in a kindly manner; clearly the visitors were moved by Madame's tears and her worries for her husband and son. They left without searching the loft thoroughly; had they done so they would have learned of the access to the other houses which would have alerted them to David's escape route.

As David gained strength his thoughts were more and more occupied by the hope that an opportunity might arise for him to cross the German lines and get back to his regiment. It must have been the hope of Julie-Celestine too, given the constant strain she was under. David had heard rumours of fugitive soldiers being smuggled across the border to Belgium and then on to Flushing in neutral Holland, before travelling to England. In fact, a clandestine network was being constructed not only to assist British soldiers but also to smuggle French and Belgians from occupied territory to England so that they could join their respective armies.

Though it was not easy, some British soldiers trapped like David had managed to escape. In Britain, readers of the *Illustrated Chronicle* on 18 May 1915 were no doubt thrilled and heartened by a story headlined: 'An Amazing Odyssey. Six Soldiers' Adventures Behind the German Lines. "In it" from Mons. Nine Months Wandering End in Escape into Holland.' Here is the story as the obviously excited journalist reported it:

There have just crossed the Belgian frontier, behind German lines, and come into Holland, six British soldiers, says the Rotterdam correspondent of the *Daily Telegraph*. Behind that plain statement lies an amazing odyssey of a battle of hairsbreadth escapes, of sufferings terrible. They were at Mons in the tragic days of August, and were cut off from their regiment in the great retreat. They crept through the encircling Germans, and for nine months have been fugitives in France and Belgium, living in fields and dugouts. They have passed through experiences probably without parallel, playing, through all these nine months, a game of hide and seek to have lost which would have meant summary execution. For a price was on their heads.

James Carrighan who (aided by a comrade called Jenkins) told me the history of the adventures said: 'It was on August 26th that the Germans got round us properly. But we managed to hide in a ditch, where we stayed all night. Next morning we found ourselves in a little paddock, only two fields away from the Germans in the middle of their lines. So we lay low all day. Then eight Frenchmen crawled up to us. We managed to keep out of sight until most of the Germans had gone on. We hid most of the time in orchards, and lived on pears for ten days. We were then a party of twenty-one, eleven English and ten French. We got to a village, making our way along the railway line and through a forest. Here we all lodged in a barn, and a woman, the best soul you ever met, brought us milk three times a day.

'The Germans, who were searching for us, were in a horse-shoe shape round the village, and were closing in on us. Private Jamieson, a scout, and a good one, took command. He got us out, nearly under the noses of twelve Uhlans. We got into a field, and stayed there for a month, with Germans only six fields away. We dug a sort of trench to hide in. The farmer gave us civilian clothes, and we worked for him in the fields for three weeks under the noses of the Germans. Then we had to clear again. We divided into three parties. My little party of eight got into a field where we made a dug-out. We lived in this for a month, stealing out at night to get food from some people in a village close by. We moved on again and tried the same plan at the next place we stopped at. It was terrible weather, raining nearly all the time. We had to keep bailing the place out nearly all night. We were pretty nearly starving some of the time. We made another trek and then lived for a month in a hut which we built in a corner of a field. Then a Belgian guided us to a village.'

The journalist had the good sense not to reveal exact locations since doing so might implicate those who had helped the soldiers, but he said they travelled openly, regularly passed German sentries and even used a train! Eventually they reached the Dutch border and now only had to get over it to reach the safety of the neutral Netherlands; but the adventure was not quite over yet for them, even with their goal so tantalisingly near:

They were lucky, but even so, they had to make three attempts to cross the frontier before the one which succeeded. Private Jenkins has scratches on his face and torn clothes, as a result of creeping through barbed wire into Holland.

One other fact worthy of record is that for the first six months the six intrepid fugitives wore their uniforms under their civilian clothes. Private Garrighan said, 'We were determined to stick to our Khaki, and for a long time had our rifles handy, because we made up our minds that we would never be taken prisoners, and that if we ran into the Germans we would die fighting. We had seen too much of their work to want to fall into their hands.'

Another escapee was Private Harry Beaumont of the 1st Royal West Kent Regiment, a reservist who was trapped under a wall collapsed by shellfire as he fell back from Mons. He was freed by locals who took him to a colliery at Wasmes, where there was a medical room, and he was treated there with other soldiers by its staff and an English-speaking engineer, Herman Capiau. As the German grip tightened he was told he would be sent to Germany as a prisoner, so he and another soldier, Arthur Heath, decided to escape, both being hidden by the Neusy family who had befriended them. Though carrying a bad leg wound, Heath left the clinic with Beaumont and made it to the Neusy home, but the next day someone from the pit said they should return. They hid in a wood, but by now it was late October and the nights were cold; in the ten days they were there Heath fell ill and Beaumont knew he had to do something so called at a café where they got a doctor, who treated Heath and returned them to the family.

Mention was made now of an escape network, but they were advised to learn some French before an attempt, so they got stuck into a dictionary given to them. Emile Neusy went often to Brussels and managed to bring back a copy of the *The Times* just before Christmas. Many visitors called and helped, but the family was wary of all comers. One was the Prince Reginald de Croy, who offered his help and the possibility of an escape, but he was disbelieved and sent away. His sister, Marie, will appear later in the story.

In February the Mayor called to say the Germans were making greater threats and asked the men to leave. Heath stayed but Beaumont moved in with another family further away, posing as a deaf and dumb relative as the house was an unofficial bar and often frequented by Germans. Shortly afterwards, the Neusy home was raided but Heath got away and turned up at his comrade's hiding place the next morning. Marie Neusy was arrested and taken to Mons. Her husband was on business in Brussels but word was sent to him by the locals so he would be prepared on his return. The couple were put on trial, but although the Germans could prove nothing about hiding escapees Mme Neusy got one month in prison for impeding the police and her husband was fined for being in possession of illicit goods.

Back into the escapees' life after six months came Herman Capiau from the mine who said an escape plan had been hatched to get them to Holland within ten days; he took their photos for forged papers, which duly turned up four days later. Beaumont was worried about an escape because he had a large Union Jack tattoo on his upper arm. A day was soon set and the first destination was to be Brussels, but this bid failed miserably when their guide missed the tram and they had to wait another four days. The Croys now played a part, and they moved off as a group with eight Irish soldiers, who caused all kinds of problems later. But the early journey to Brussels via Mons went well and they were housed in a clinic run by an English nurse they later discovered was Edith Cavell. She preferred them to stay indoors, and although she could not order them to do so, she insisted that if they went out they kept a low profile and returned by 9 pm. On one occasion the Irish broke their curfew and got into a drunken brawl in a bar; everyone then had to be moved hastily from the clinic to other safe houses.

It was decided that they would be moved in pairs; Heath and Beaumont were split up and Beaumont found himself with another Irishman called Michael Carey, who had reason to know just what capture would mean, as will be recounted later. On 6 April 1915 a guide whom Beaumont immediately distrusted picked them up with four of the other Irishmen, and they headed off, travelling through Louvain and staying overnight at an abbey at Averbode. Another scare came courtesy of the Irish when two of them started fighting just past a sentry point. One had discovered that the other had English letters on him which would have doomed them all. The letters were taken from him and destroyed. They reached Turnhout, where their initial guide passed them to another with the address of a safe house where they would stay overnight, but Beaumont's misgivings proved correct and they found it was full of Germans. Sadly, they returned the 20 miles to the abbey, where they were disguised as monks for a week's wait.

The next attempt saw Beaumont and Carey again make it to Brussels, where they were split from the others and lodged in a house which offered them the first bath they could remember, along with lavish food and alcohol. Three other soldiers were there, two Frenchmen and a man who claimed to be Canadian and whom Beaumont greatly distrusted. Their next destination was Antwerp with the Frenchmen, led by another guide, but while they made it through a checkpoint, their French comrades did not and were arrested. Their guide, the same one who had led them to Turnhout, left them at a hotel saying he would return the next day to pay and move them on; it came as no surprise when the next day he failed to appear. They were in trouble as the owner was demanding payment and they had no money. But they remembered spotting an American Relief office, which offered the funds and a new guide, but warned them it might be a while before they could move.

On 16 May they were told that tomorrow would be the day, but they were warned that it would not be easy as the 12-mile route was well patrolled, with at least two lines of sentries to cross as well as a partly electrified wire and a moated border. Their new, elderly, guide did not inspire confidence either, but they had to trust him and he turned out to be both canny and swift. In three hours they reached the border, where, alarmingly, he ordered them to strip naked and throw their bundled clothes over the wire; they then crawled underneath and through the dykes and finally ran for it. Luckily, it was a foul night which might have kept any German guards indoors, and shortly they were in Holland, chatting to a Dutch border soldier who seemed to know the old man well; they were soon moved to a café for something to eat and drink.

As Beaumont was in 'civvies' and not military uniform he would not be interned by the authorities and he was passed on to the British Consul at Flushing who gave him funds and said he would be put onto a boat to Britain from Rotterdam. Waiting in a hotel, he was delighted to see Heath's name in the register and they had a reunion the next day. Five other soldiers were awaiting repatriation too. Heath had made it across to Holland hidden in a hay cart. They sailed for home overnight, and dawn found them tied up at Tilbury on the Thames waiting for their pilot boat, but they were taken off for questioning by intelligence officers and then back to his unit. Beaumont continued to serve but never went overseas again.

None of this could have been known at the Baudhuin home, but Julie-Celestine also worried that any attempt by David to find his way through the German lines would be impossible and could have disastrous results. David, however, was adamant that a way should be found for him to escape. He was restless and longed to be able to get out of the confines of this small house to breathe some fresh air and get some exercise. It was the lack of these in part which was having a growing effect on his health, and to the alarm of the family he fell ill again, leading to another call on the services of Dr Tison. The doctor's indifference to risk was shared by the faithful Nurse Mutin, and under their collective care the patient once more rallied, but Dr Tison now had some further medical advice.

The doctor insisted that if he were to stay healthy David must get more exercise and fresh air if possible, but he must have been aware of the difficulty which went with this prescription. Just how could a fugitive British soldier possibly take exercise? The streets were full of Germans and secret police who simply sat around in cafés or wandered the streets and markets eavesdropping. Julie-Celestine was also aware that in a small town like Le Cateau everyone knew each other very well and outsiders were soon spotted and noted.

But Julie-Celestine equally knew that the doctor was right and a young man could not spend all his time indoors. She was a resourceful woman and after some careful thought decided that, dyed black and with a few simple alterations, David's uniform could pass as a local working man's clothing which, with caution, would allow him to leave the house during the hours of darkness. With Léon to guide him he would be able to get the exercise he not only craved but also badly needed. They would have to go out after the curfew, keep to the quietest streets and always be aware of the possibility of running into German patrols. But it had to be done and so, soon after the decision was made and his clothes were altered, David got his first taste of freedom in several months; he must have found it wonderfully exhilarating.

This arrangement, as far as it went, was satisfactory for the time being, but David still harboured the idea of escaping from the occupied region and returning to his regiment. Therefore, during his nocturnal trips out and about with Léon he sought a potential route out of the town. Sadly, they found the Germans to be well organized in the positioning of sentries and the regularity of patrols. During the early days and weeks of the war it had been possible, with assistance, often from poachers and smugglers, for fugitives to escape from the clutches of the enemy; but now, in late 1914, the gaps had been closed and security tightened. There were a number of successful escapes but also many failures, which often resulted in the soldiers and their helpers being executed. Many of the smuggling routes into Belgium had been discovered and it was now almost impossible even to reach the border.

Just how dangerous was proved to two other soldiers who, like David, had lost their units after Le Cateau. Teaming up, Private Robert Digby of the 1st Hampshire Regiment and Private John Sligo of the 1st Somerset Light Infantry found themselves near the village of Villeret, 22 miles from Le Cateau. Unfortunately, it was occupied by the enemy and they were spotted by some German cavalry, who soon saddled up and gave chase, firing at the escapees as they tried to make it to nearby woods. Both men were wounded, the older Sligo more severely, and when the younger and fitter Digby made it into the cover of the trees he turned to see the riders catch up with his comrade and shoot him dead. Sligo's body was buried in Villeret churchyard and Digby went back on the run, but after several days he again found himself not far away, now with another eight stragglers. We will return to their story later.

While David was unaware of their specific fates, he had heard rumours of British and French stragglers getting aid to escape, and hope was raised further by a neighbour of Julie-Celestine, M Joseph-Cyrille Gosse, who said he might be able to help. The account in *Chambers Journal* records: 'Gosse was known by his intimates to be involved in what was called patriotic activities on behalf of the allies. It was said that he was associated with the Alice network which was headed by Louise de Bettignies who was based in Lille'. Was this network headed by the remarkable Louise de Bettignies the lifeline that David had been waiting for?

Louise de Bettignies was born in Saint-Amand-les-Eaux in 1880, the daughter of Henri de Bettignies and Julienne Mabille de Poncheville. Henri had sold the family business due to financial difficulties shortly before her birth, but despite the family's reduced circumstances, Louise was taught the values of her peers and got a good education in Valenciennes. Strongly religious, she followed her sister by spending time in a Carmelite convent before becoming a housekeeper with English and German families, as much as anything to improve her language skills and to see more of Europe. At the war's outbreak Louise assisted in the defence of Bethune by helping to supply the besieged town. In February 1915 she was approached by a French officer suggesting she become an intelligence agent, an offer soon repeated by the British. Seeking spiritual advice from her priest, Father Boulenge, who called her the 'Joan of Arc of the North', she agreed. She took the operational name of Alice Dubois and began to develop the foundations in Lille of what was to become 'Service Alice' or 'Service Ramble'.

Louise was able to pass information to the British by travelling through Belgium into Holland. She was joined in the spring of 1915 by a young woman from Roubaix named Marie-Léonine Vanhoutte, alias Charlotte Lameron, who had since August 1914 worked with medical relief and ambulances. Service Alice grew to employ eighty people, operating in two divisions. The first was made up of observers and couriers placed at strategic locations near the Belgian border to watch troop movements. So effective were they that information could be passed to the British authorities within twenty-four hours. The second arm of the network was based around Lille, where information could be gathered in sensitive areas on enemy numbers and movements, artillery battery positions or storage areas. The network also had access to a laboratory provided to them by M and Mme Geyter, where they could reproduce maps, plans and photographs, all vital to the Allied war effort.

Louise also worked under the pseudonym 'Pauline' and it was as Pauline that she provided useful information which resulted in the destruction of artillery in 1915 at Carency and Loos-en-Gohelle. During the summer of 1915 the network was extended to cover the area around Cambrai, Valenciennes, Saint-Quentin and Mézières, and by autumn had passed on information about preparations for the battle of Verdun. It was around this time that Alice and Charlotte began to feel they were being watched. On 24 September 1915 Marie-Léonine Vanhoutte was arrested following a meeting in Brussels and taken to the Saint-Gilles prison. Louise was later arrested, together with her driver Georges de Saever, in Tournai on 20 October whilst attempting to cross into France.

Louise and Marie-Léonine were reunited within the confines of the Saint-Gilles prison on 26 October. During six months of questioning Louise gave nothing away, saying little and denying everything. The Germans were unable to establish any certain link between Louise de Bettignies and Alice Dubois but they coerced a compatriot, Louise Letellier, into giving a confession and obtained five damning letters from Louise/Alice.

On 16 March 1916, the German war council based in Brussels, which included General von Bissing and war adviser Dr Stoeber, sentenced Louise de Bettignies to death for espionage, though without being able to prove that she was head of the network. Her sentence was commuted to life imprisonment, possibly due to the local good repute of the Bettignies family or the outcry that had followed the execution of Nurse Edith Cavell. In a statement she made in German, the only time she spoke the language during her trial, she acknowledged her role but begged for clemency for Marie-Léonie Vanhoutte and Georges de Saever. They were initially sentenced to death, but this was commuted to fifteen years hard labour for treason during wartime by aiding espionage. The two women were sent to Siegburg prison near Cologne, but Louise died on 17 September 1918 of complications from surgery on a pleural abscess and was buried at Bocklemund cemetery in Westfriedhof.

On 21 February 1920 her body was repatriated and on 16 March 1920 a tribute was organized in Lille during which the 'Joan of Arc of the North' was posthumously awarded the Légion d'Honneur, the Croix du Guerre and the 1914–18 medal with palm and British honours. Louise de Bettignies is buried in Saint-Amand-les-Eaux cemetery. Armistice Day 1927 saw the unveiling of statues of her on Boulevard Carnot in Lille and in the Chapel at Notre-Dame de Lorette near Arras, in the middle of her nation's largest war cemetery. The wooden cross from her original grave in Germany, together with her mention in dispatches letter, are also displayed there.

A friend of Louise de Bettignies and another major player in hiding and trying to rescue soldiers trapped behind the lines was Louise Thuliez. She had been born in the Nord department of France in 1881 and was working as a teacher at Saint Waast-la-Vallée close to the Belgian border when the war broke out. She was soon involved in what she saw as her duty of helping stranded soldiers, along with a local noblewoman, Princesse Marie of Croy. She acted as a driver and was friendly with the English nurse Edith Cavell, aiming always to get men to neutral Holland. But Mme Thuliez was betrayed, arrested by the Germans at the end of July 1915 and sent to a prison in Brussels along with Louise de Bettignies. At her trial, which took place in October, she was initially condemned to death, but the King of Spain intervened and pleaded for clemency and she was instead sentenced to prison with hard labour, also at Siegburg.

After the war the British government awarded her an OBE and she returned to teaching, but also wrote a best-selling account of her adventures which was also published in English as *Condemned to Death*. When the Germans occupied her country again in 1940, she took issue with them for a second time, setting up an escape route to England and supporting local resistance groups. This time she managed to stay out of the clutches of the enemy. This redoubtable woman, who also received medals from her own government and from America, died in Paris in 1966. Her home village of Preux aux Bois erected a statue of her in 1970 and a street was named after her in Paris four years later.

Back in Le Cateau, Gosse told David that he would help him escape and he thought that his contacts in the Alice network would be able to assist. Gosse promised that he would let him know when the arrangements had been made. David was delighted, but his joy did not last long; his hopes were dashed only days later, when it was learned that Gosse and his wife had been arrested by the enemy in the most unlucky circumstances. The German police had gone to Gosse's house on routine enquires and had left their horses tethered outside. After questioning the couple they got ready to leave, but on reaching the door of the house Mme Gosse saw that the horses had eaten all of her beloved plants. She was furious and began rebuking the two policemen for their carelessness in leaving their horses so close. During her tirade a pigeon was seen to fly into the loft in the attic of their house. Now the Germans had something to pin on them and acted immediately. Both husband and wife were arrested under suspicion of keeping carrier pigeons to send information to the Allies. The possibility that this couple had been sending intelligence to the enemy meant that there could be only one sentence for this offence, as has already been seen. Gosse and his wife were swiftly tried, found guilty of the charges, sentenced to death and duly executed by firing squad.

A proclamation was posted in Le Cateau on 24 November informing the population of the execution of Joseph-Cyrille and Clemence Gosse; its clear intention, as well as to inform, was to intimidate the local population, for it went on to warn all inhabitants of the seriousness of possessing carrier pigeons, arms or ammunition. All such items must be declared and handed over to the occupiers by 1300 hrs on 26 November. Anyone found in possession after this time would be shot *sans autre formalité*, or without trial.

With his established clandestine contacts throughout the region and across the border in Belgium, Gosse had been David's best, indeed only realistic, chance of getting away; without his expert knowledge and assistance escape would now be impossible. These executions also highlighted, not only to David and the whole Baudhuin family but to all of those who were in the clutches of the German army, the devastation that would be wrought on anyone caught defying the German rules. The occupiers intended to keep the population in check by any method necessary and no resistance to their dominance would be accepted or tolerated.

Incredibly, it was on the day of the execution of Gosse and his wife that another fugitive left the Le Cateau area trying to make his way towards the safety of British lines. Private Patrick Fowler of 11th Hussars and two others had also become trapped after the battle on 26 August. They had ridden around lost, but it soon became clear that they were the wrong side of the lines as they caught glimpses of enemy gun positions and observed the roads were full of German convoys. Hiding themselves was difficult enough but their horses were impossible to conceal, so they left them with a farmer who agreed to feed them. They split up to try and improve their chances, but Fowler could find no way through. He was now in a tight spot as he was alone, spoke no French and was terrified by the sight of every living soul – but he was still a trained soldier, whose survival skills now kicked in. Always erring on the side of caution, he avoided all contact but managed to get by and took each day as it came. Incredibly, he survived hidden in the woods and living on his wits for almost five months, until in January 1915 he was found in an exhausted state by Louis Basquin. His discoverer proved to be a sympathetic and exceptional man who, despite the language difficulties, managed to lead Fowler to a haystack to hide and made him understand that he would return with food and drink. By this time Fowler was in a very poor way, completely dishevelled, dressed in his ragged uniform and an old civilian coat. His hands and face were covered in dried blood from the cuts and scratches he had acquired crawling into the deepest thickets to try and avoid discovery. He was bearded, filthy and very undernourished.

Basquin and his wife lived in a tiny house in the nearby village of Bertry and it was, he knew immediately, far too small to hide anyone. He had made his mind up that he must do something for Fowler as he was sure to die of exposure if he was left where he was without shelter in the freezing winter weather. Basquin decided to consult his redoubtable and wise mother-in-law, Mme Belmont-Gobert, who lived in the same village. Mme Belmont-Gobert had her daughter Angèle living with her, while another daughter, Euphemie, was in unoccupied France. The family was one of the poorest in the village, living only on what young Angèle earned from her sewing and embroidery. Even in normal times they had a very tough life. Now under German occupation food was even scarcer, strictly rationed and expensive, and the penalties they would face if caught harbouring this British soldier would be severe. Would they be prepared to put their lives at risk for a foreign soldier? They did not take long to come up with the answer, for they knew well that this foreigner had fought to save France and that his life was threatened not only by the common foe but also by the cruel winter weather.

Patrick Fowler was born in Dublin and had worked as a labourer before joining the army as full-time soldier before his nineteenth birthday in 1896, having spent some time as volunteer with the 5th battalion of the Royal Dublin Fusiliers. He joined the Hussars, was posted to its 8th battalion initially, then two years later was transferred to the 11th. Fowler clearly took to soldiering, spending some time in India, and in 1901 agreed to extend his service to a twelve-year stint, duly qualifying for the award of medals for Long Service and Good Conduct and pocketing a no doubt welcome £5 as a gratuity.

On the outbreak of the war he was quickly sent to France with his unit and they were soon in action. His service papers, among the few to escape destruction or damage by the Luftwaffe in the London Blitz of the Second World War, make interesting reading. His Casualty Form Active Service paper states that he was lost 'in the field' on or about 26 August 1914. However, it is not until 16 September that this status is amended to that of missing presumed dead on or about that earlier date. Then, on the line below dated 24 December 1915, the form states that the War Office has accepted that he is dead for official purposes. Another paper in his dossier states that a pension is now being paid to his wife. The dossier gives some idea of the timescale by which news must have reached families like the Cruikshanks back in Glasgow. Many service papers must have contained similar bald facts, but Fowler's were to receive some amazing additions.

Fowler, however, was not the only British soldier being helped by the villagers of Bertry. Indeed, more remarkably, he was not even the only man from his regiment! Another patriotic French family was protecting Corporal Herbert Hull, who like Fowler had been separated from the 11th Hussars after Le Cateau. He had been found by a local called Gustave Cardon collapsed on the battlefield, but had revived when Cardon gave him wine from his flask. He then hid the injured soldier provisionally and promised to return for him after nightfall and lead him to a place of safety. Cardon had been expecting his army call up and, having registered at the outbreak of war, had been ordered to go back home to await official orders – something he realized was not likely to happen now, since the Germans were in occupation of his village. So Cardon had decided that if he could not serve the French Army, he would help its British allies, and now he had been given a chance to do so in the shape of this soldier he had discovered.

Major General Sir Edward Spears, a leading British liaison officer and later one of the war's finest contemporary chroniclers, wrote of Cardon: 'In spite of his tribulations, in spite of the sufferings of his family, he never regretted having taken home the British soldier he found in a collapsed state on the battlefield of Le Cateau.' He described how the Frenchman said he felt he was only 'obeying the voice of his conscience' and was immediately and fully aware of the risks he ran as he carried Hull to his cottage and arranged a clever cache in a small loft. Spears, a fluent French speaker and a Francophile, was to play a very important part in this story and will reappear later. We will also hear more of the fates of Fowler, Hull and their protectors, but they were all to have an impact on David back in Le Cateau.

David's hiding place in the Baudhuin loft, with its easy access to adjoining properties through the roof space, had already saved him more than once. Further surprise searches had been made, but each time he had been quick-witted and swift enough to evade them. However, the seemingly ever more frequent visits and questions to Julie-Celestine made her certain that she was under suspicion and there would be more calls and searches. So far the family's luck had held, but how long could they remain so fortunate?

Chapter 6

Coming Out

David was by now very much a family member, and because a few close friends and neighbours were in on the secret he also had a small support group, all of whom in one way or another assisted Julie-Celestine in looking after him. He had settled into a routine of staying in during the day and going out for short periods occasionally during the hours of darkness. For David, however, these short excursions were never enough, and he was soon chafing for more freedom. As the ruse had gone undetected by the Germans, he started to become confident that there ought to be a solution. There was – but one he surely could never have thought of alone.

Close to the Baudhuins' home was the house of Mme Adrienne Place; she had a young and attractive niece, Aimée Olivier, who had been entrusted with the secret, often brought tobacco to David and spent time chatting with him. They were of similar age, Aimée being two years younger. She was a friendly girl with an engaging smile and almost immediately she and David became close friends which was no great surprise to anyone; indeed, Aimée was to become a major influence in David's life.

David's desire for more freedom was no longer hampered by the wounds he had received, and following the care lavished on him by Julie-Celestine he was almost back to full fitness. Days spent in the tiny house were boring and frustrating for him. He still harboured hopes that a way could be found for him to escape through the German lines and get back to territory held by the BEF or the French. But as the weeks and months passed, and as further restrictions were put in place by the occupiers, his hopes of freedom began to drain away. The German forces in Le Cateau were increasing in number and their demands upon the townspeople were growing daily. The times of patrols and troop movements were unpredictable, and there were always Germans going to and from their billets throughout the town. Because of this it was becoming more and more difficult for

David to venture out in his makeshift disguise, even under the cloak of darkness.

Men were regularly stopped and questioned in the street by German patrols or police, but women much less often. And so an idea came to mind: what about dressing David as a woman? In a 1921 interview David claimed the idea was his, as he was of slight build, fresh-faced and beardless. It was a crazy idea – in fact, it was so crazy it might just work. Julie-Celestine had a nephew who was a hairdresser, from whom she acquired a wig, whilst Nurse Mutin brought women's clothes and shoes to the Baudhuin house. It must have seemed a strange affair to David, but it shows how desperate he was to gain some freedom.

Feeling strange in these clothes, David presented himself to Aimée and the Baudhuin family for inspection. Aimée's response to seeing David promenading around the small room was to comment that although he did indeed look like a woman he acted like a man; his mannerisms and movements were too masculine, the way he walked and his gestures were all wrong. There was a lot of work to be done if David was to present himself to the town as a young lady without raising the suspicions of the Germans.

It took time, but David was keen to learn and Aimée was happy to spend hours teaching him. One problem they faced was adapting the length of the young Scotsman's stride from a manly pace to something more female. It was clever Aimée who came up with the brilliant solution of tying a string to David's ankles and adjusting the length until she was satisfied the stride was just right. The impatient young man was keen to test his disguise as soon as possible, but Aimée was adamant that he had to be perfect in every way before facing the dangers of the street and the occupying troops. At last it was agreed that he should take his first cautious steps outside dressed as a woman during the evening, as darkness was drawing in.

It must have taken a great deal of courage for Aimée to walk out on to the streets of Le Cateau accompanying a British soldier dressed in female attire. The town was full of Germans and who could say whom they might stumble into around any corner? Perhaps it was the confidence of youth, or its foolishness, that spurred them on. Julie-Celestine had become a surrogate mother to David, but he felt suffocated by the long days with nothing to occupy or to stimulate him. The time spent with Aimée had become his only pleasure, and he soon came to long for her visits, although they were never really alone together as there was always one or more members of the Baudhuin family present in the cramped house.

One can hardly imagine David's excitement as he finally stepped into the narrow street in his disguise. It was an adventure in more ways than one, but there could not be even the slightest mistake. He did not want to appear too cautious or do anything else likely to bring attention on himself or Aimée. He need not have worried, however, for he played his female role to perfection, with care at first, but as time moved on and he developed greater confidence, becoming more and more comfortable in his disguise and demeanour. In fact, the scheme was a great success, and so 'Mademoiselle Louise' was born.

Going out in such a way was undoubtedly reckless when it was known that the Germans were obsessed with the idea of hidden British soldiers in the area. One incident recorded in the diary kept by M Laforest, who lived on Rue Fénélon, bears vivid witness to this. On 14 January 1915 he noted:

A drunk inhabitant of Le Cateau, a roofer living on Rue Seydoux, was at the Lanniaux bar and was talking about the Englishmen who were hidden in houses since the battle of Le Cateau. He took no notice of a German who was seated nearby pretending to read but who understood a little French; the German immediately left to alert his commanding officer to the fact that there were Englishmen hidden in the house; he had misunderstood. Straight away, sixteen men with fixed bayonets burst into the bar. Two sentries were posted at the door and absolutely nobody was allowed out. Lanniaux, who was ill and in bed, was forced to prove that he was not English by showing his portrait displayed in the house. The neighbouring houses were searched also.

News of events like this spread quickly through the town and ratcheted up the concerns of the hidden and their guardians.

In a 1921 interview for the magazine *Sous Leur Griffes* (In Their Clutches), David recalled some of his adventures during his time in Le Cateau:

To begin with I went out walking one evening with my friend. We met a lot of Germans. My disguise was perfect as they didn't seem to suspect my true identity. On the contrary, they seemed rather friendly, but replying to them wasn't on our agenda.

This first success spurred him on, and from the next day onwards he went out often. After two or three attempts he no longer feared being recognized. Little could David have known at this point that his female 'alter ego' would remain a feature of his life for two years. All the same, he could not see a way of reaching the British lines. A number of people in Le Cateau knew that 'Mademoiselle Louise' was really a British soldier, but the secret was well kept. One person, however, who had guessed the truth behind his disguise without his knowing, was to present a danger to him later on. This person, only known as 'Madame D', was now in German pay as an informer. Patriots would call these traitors *'Mauvais Français'* (bad French).

David had already met Madame D in the streets of Le Cateau weeks earlier when, escaping from the Germans, he found himself on her doorstep and she arrived carrying a bucket of water. A bullet meant for him had gone through the bucket, while another made a hole in her clothes and skimmed her leg. The encounter had clearly made an impression on her, something David was convinced of when, meeting him in the street while in disguise, she told him she knew that he was no woman but a British soldier hiding from the Germans. Worse still, this woman was very attentive and seemed actually to have fallen for him, or so she said. He managed to get rid of her for the time being by saying he was not interested, but the encounter must have set alarm bells ringing. It had every reason to do so. For despite his indifference to her, Madame D continued to bother him every time the occasion presented itself. This continued for almost two years, but one evening, when he refused to talk to her, she became angry and threatened revenge. 'At the time I had no idea that she was secretly working for the Germans and took no notice of her threats, and besides she didn't immediately follow up her threats,' David recalled.

During these two years he had several amusing adventures. Judging by the way they looked at him, the German soldiers he met in the town and its vicinity seemed to find 'Mademoiselle Louise' attractive. One should bear in mind that they were mostly young men, away from home and living with the fear that they could be killed in battle at any time. They would take their pleasures where they could find them. The allure of French *mesdemoiselles* would undoubtedly have been very appealing. David must have been aware of this and the dangers it presented, but he seems to have played it just about right. As he worded it himself in an interview: 'Naturally I avoided their advances, although it wasn't always easy to shake off their attentions. On a certain occasion, however, my *chic* appearance served me well.'

The occasion was this. David was walking in the street in nearby Bazuel with a young lady and her baby. As there were many Germans in the village, he had asked the young mother to allow him to take the pram and he pushed it in front of him, behaving in a typically French manner, bending towards the sleeping boy and sweetly cooing to him. The aim in taking the child with them in the pram was to try to bring back hidden food; they had very little then and any opportunity to acquire extra had to be explored. They had succeeded in obtaining some butter and eggs, and having heard that a cow had been slaughtered in a nearby farm a few days before, hoped to add a little meat to their provisions. The farmer knew the young lady and so they had managed to get a piece of paunch of beef. The difficulty was transporting it home without attracting the attention of the Germans.

During the war the French proved themselves to be most ingenious in fooling the enemy. Thus on this occasion David and his companion hung the bag containing the piece of beef tripe underneath the pram, hoping that if the Germans asked to inspect it they would only look inside and not underneath. The strategy was a perfect success for most of their journey but almost came unstuck at a crucial moment.

David remembered it well: 'At the precise moment that a few Krauts approached us, we noticed with great apprehension that the water was leaking out of the bag that contained the beef tripe and was leaving a tell-tale trace on the path behind us.' Thinking quickly, he resorted to turning on a bit of 'feminine' charm to avoid having what they held so dear taken from them – or even worse. David played the timid young lady and when the Germans came close gave them his most ingratiating smile. The soldiers fell for it and, he added, would have accorded them anything they asked for, but he and his companion were more than happy to be able to continue on their way having avoided tragedy.

But this was not to be the end of their dangers or adventures for that day. They still had a way to go to get their illicit delicacy home, and quite soon afterwards, as a result of its bumpy ride, the bag containing the beef tripe came undone at just the moment when they had to cross a bridge guarded by two German sentries. The situation was serious. They were exposing themselves to severe punishment just for having procured black market goods, though if the contraband was discovered this would have been the least of their worries. David remembered: 'Of course, we could have hidden the provisions somewhere and so escaped the sanction, but we might not have been able to retrieve them later and we had resolved not to sacrifice the delicious dinner we had planned upon.'

More quick thinking was needed, and David just had time to murmur to his companion to go around the pram and attach the parcel to that side. For his part, he sought to draw the attention of the sentries to himself. 'With the gracious smile I addressed them, the expressions of these "brave" Germans who had looked incensed at the sight of the revealing package quickly brightened.' He recalled adopting his most ingratiating manner: 'I went towards them, addressing them a smile which, according to my friends, would soften the hardest of heart.' The sentries, delighted by this mark of fawning to them by such a charming French girl, responded with a salute and let 'her' know that they hoped they would have the pleasure of meeting 'her' again later when they were off duty. If only they had known!

All this charm from the smiling Mademoiselle Louise had the Germans eating of out 'her' hand. But the real lady, David's companion and partner in crime, also played her part perfectly by oozing sweetness and innocence. Blushing, she explained the contents of the package and told them how much she would like to get home without any trouble. David came to her aid, still using his most gracious smile. He bowed timidly and murmured in as perfect French as possible that they 'seemed too good and too generous soldiers to bother us'. As a result, they straightened with pride before this compliment and declared she need not worry about her provisions, they would not say a word. He added, 'In the end, they helped my companion to attach the package back onto the pram again.'

David had clearly become very confident in his disguise and felt that he could freely walk the streets of the town without raising the suspicions of the occupying German soldiers or police. The outings now became a regular part of his daily routine. His command of the local patois was also improving, and while he knew the locals would realize he was not one of them, the ears of the Germans were not fine-tuned enough to spot the difference in his accent. There were still serious dangers to be avoided, but Mademoiselle Louise was blending in and became an ever commoner sight in the streets of Le Cateau. He usually went out with Aimée, and they would do all the customary things that young ladies of the time would be expected to. Food was scarce and expensive, but they queued with others at market stalls and in the shops to acquire whatever meagre rations were available at a price they could afford.

In February 1915, when David had been hidden for six months, came distressing news in another German proclamation telling of the capture and execution of eleven British soldiers who had been hiding at a mill in Iron-en-Thierache, only a few miles south-east of Le Cateau. Not only had the soldiers been shot but one of their protectors, M Vincent Chalandre, had suffered the same fate. The men had been sheltered by the mill-owning Logez family and at a nearby house owned by the Chalandres, and the two families had agreed to feed them. There was talk of escape, but the Germans were occupying the area in strength. On 15 December 1914, without warning, forty Germans arrived at the mill. Mme Léonie Logez delayed them long enough for her daughter, Jeanne, to warn the British soldiers. Her courage managed to buy them just enough time to flee by wading through the icy waters of the river to a nearby copse. The Germans surrounded the mill but a thorough search found nothing incriminating. According to Herbert Walton's article 'The Secret of the Mill', published ten years after the war, the soldiers had used this escape route on several occasions when under threat of discovery.

Mme Logez was their principal source of food. As well as running the mill, alone since her husband had suffered a stroke, she was a smallholder with a few cows. She held a trader's pass issued by the occupiers which allowed her to move around the area selling her wares. She smuggled food to the soldiers hidden in her milk buckets, often taking them soup and bread.

For six months the fugitives were able to keep their presence a secret, but they were betrayed by jealousy. There was a woman in the village called Blanche Maréchal, who, although married, offered her services to several local men as well as the occupying troops. One of her lovers was sixteen-year-old Clovis, Vincent Chalandre's son, and another was a Franco-Prussian war veteran named Bachelet, fifty years his senior. Clovis, described as 'a stupid youth' in one account, had been indiscreet during an intimate moment with the woman, telling her about the British soldiers at the mill. The woman then told her husband, who spread the gossip further. Bachelet lodged in a *brasserie*, and in a fit of jealousy on the evening of 21 February Clovis threw stones at the older man's window. A furious Bachelet shouted to the boy, 'You'll pay for this. Tomorrow I am going to inform on you and the English – you will all be shot!' Clovis went home but through stupidity or fear told no one of the threat.

The next morning, Bachelet went to the German headquarters in Guise, where he was received by senior officers who recorded his statement denouncing not only the British soldiers but all the locals sheltering them. Strangely, on the same morning Mme Logez attended the headquarters to renew her trading pass. It was normally granted without question, but on this occasion the Germans were less helpful and informed her that she would have to wait there until the evening as the HQ staff were very busy. She actually spotted Bachelet through an open door talking to Kommandant Waechter; when Bachelet saw her, he said he would say no more in front of her.

With this information the Germans sent a patrol to the mill, arriving so quickly that there was no time to warn the British soldiers, who were caught and arrested together with members of both families. The Germans then proceeded to burn down first the house and then the mill. *'Elle a aussi mérité la mort'* (she also deserves death) appeared on the official announcement of Mme Logez's conviction, but in fact the court martial sentenced Mme Logez and Jeanne to imprisonment in Germany, along with Mme Germaine Chalandre, her daughter Germaine and son Clovis. The sick and distressed Monsieur Logez was turned adrift, homeless and unable to look after himself, and died soon afterwards. Mme Chalandre remained in prison until the Armistice and having suffered from ill health during her imprisonment she too died soon after her release.

There was one British survivor of this tragic incident. Twelve members of the Munster Fusiliers were hiding at Iron, but Private Michael Carey had spent the night with friends elsewhere in the village and so was not present when the Germans raided. When he visited the still smouldering ruins of the mill, villagers said he threw himself to his knees, thanked God for his survival and also prayed for his comrades. Carey continued to be hidden and was then put on the Dutch escape route, where he was teamed up with Harry Beaumont; together they made it to Holland and then home.

The new proclamation was designed to spread fear and to impress on the local population exactly what their fate would be should they offer help to British soldiers. It stated: 'Let this be a warning to people of the region who are sheltering men of the enemy forces. They will be condemned to death.' The vigilance of the occupiers had been heightened by these events, and even though Julie-Celestine had known from the minute she took David into her home what would happen if she was caught, this proclamation was a forceful reminder of the dangerous path she was following.

The discovery and execution of the soldiers at the mill was quickly followed by renewed attempts on the part of the Germans to flush out other enemy servicemen being hidden in the occupied region. Julie-Celestine's house was again searched, and yet again David was able to conceal himself in a neighbouring cellar, where he was compelled to stay until nightfall. The faithful and resourceful Léon managed to sneak into the cellar to keep David updated on events. The attitude of the Germans on this search had been much more threatening than on previous occasions, as they were sure Mme Baudhuin was hoodwinking them.

This worrying upsurge of activity meant that David's partial liberty had to be curtailed, at least until things settled down as everyone in the town hoped they would, and Julie-Celestine decided that David had to be moved to another hiding place. Despite her deep worries she was determined that her young Scottish soldier had to be protected at all costs.

So David's female clothes were sent to the cellar with a message to disguise himself and meet a friend of hers on a street corner after dark. This friend had a house on the other side of town, and David would be lodged in her cellar. Although David was now well practised in posing as a girl, the tension as they walked through the town must have been terrific. They passed a number of Germans, any one of whom would have been amazed if they had been told that the demure young girl strolling with the older woman was really an enemy soldier. This friend kept him hidden for three weeks until she told David that her home was to become a billet for occupying troops, so he would have to move again. Dressed as Louise, he again crossed the town back to the Baudhuin house. Now David still went out in disguise, but very cautiously and less often than before. He spent more time in the Baudhuin living room by day and at night slept in his uncomfortable loft hideaway or, on occasions, shared Léon's bedroom.

One day as Julie-Celestine was washing there came a pounding on the door of the house; it was another German search. David was in the back room with Léon and had no time to dash for the loft. There are two recorded versions of what happened next. According to the first, Julie-Celestine pushed David into the linen chest and threw a blanket over him. As the patrol came in she stood in front of the chest and railed at them: 'Why do you come here again and again? You know I have nothing to hide. There is no money to buy black market food yet you keep coming back.'

The Germans were taken aback as normally she kept her temper and held her tongue. 'We search all of the houses, Madame' replied one, as men went to the other rooms.

She sat on the linen box and began to sob. 'This is too much. We have nothing but still you want more from us.'

Léon knelt beside his distraught mother with his arm around her shoulders. She could hear the Germans tramping around her meagre home opening cupboards and drawers. She knew the routine well by now and realized it would not take them long to satisfy themselves that there was little here to interest them.

Her sobbing continued. 'Take anything you want, take it all, leave us to starve! Will you turn us out into the fields like animals?'

The Germans were making for the front door now. 'Do not be

foolish enough to try to hide anything from us, Madame,' said one, 'for we will return.'

In the second account, David was hidden in a washing boiler with wet clothes thrown on top of him. As the Germans searched, Julie-Celestine said to Léon, 'Help me to take this back to a house across the road.' She told the Germans that this neighbour had left when the town was occupied and that she was now hanging her washing out there. One of the searchers peered into the boiler but saw only the washing. On finishing their search they ordered her to take them to the other house, but by then David had got clear and was drying himself off elsewhere.

Seven months after the Guise executions further terrible news came to the ears of the people of Le Cateau. It arrived in the form of an announcement that a woman in Bertry had been caught with a British soldier her family had been protecting in their home. The married woman, Marie-Louise Cardon, was a young friend of Julie-Celestine, and the soldier was another 11th Hussar, Corporal Herbert Hull, who had been found on the battlefield between the towns of Bertry and Troisvilles by her husband, Gustave. Apparently, Hull had a smattering of French and had told Cardon that he dreaded no fate except that of being taken prisoner by the Germans.

Londoner Herbert Hull's army papers have not survived, but in Census records he first appears at home aged eight in 1891 as a schoolboy. The family business was tailoring, and in the 1901 Census nineteen-year-old Herbert is recorded as living at home on Leytonstone Road in the East End with his parents, George and Clara in their early fifties, siblings Clara, George and William in their twenties and a younger brother, Alfred. All worked in the rag trade. In 1911, Herbert is still at home with his parents at Kitchener Road, Upton Lane, Forest Gate, Upton, London, and the family business is still going, with unmarried Herbert working as a clothier's cutter. Sometime after this he must have fancied a change and enlisted. By 1914 he had proved himself an able soldier, earning two stripes as a corporal. His Medal Index Card lists his rank, number and medal entitlements and states that he entered France on 15 August 1914 and was presumed dead eleven days later. But the authorities did not then have all the facts.

On the night of Hull's rescue, Cardon returned and led him to the family home in Bertry, where he and his wife kept him. Like David

Cruickshank, he was hidden in the loft of their tiny house, the entrance to which was a small trapdoor in the ceiling, concealed with whitewashed sacking so well that only the closest inspection would reveal it. For thirteen months the soldier was hidden and cared for, and it is doubtful that Hull would ever have been found by the Germans but for a local woman, Irma Ferlicot, who was in their pay. She roamed the town listening to conversations and soaking up any rumours. It is easy to imagine the difficulty of keeping secrets in a small community, especially if you had an enemy soldier to feed with no ration allowance. Friends had to be trusted in providing for the basic needs of the fugitive. A close neighbour of the Cardons heard they had a British soldier in their loft. Ferlicot soon became aware too, paid this woman 400 francs for the information and betrayed Hull and the Cardons to the Germans.

Hull was arrested on 27 September 1915 after troops burst into the house and went straight to the loft, tearing away the whitewashed sacking that had camouflaged the trapdoor. Hull, unlike David, had no access to the roof space of the next door houses and was trapped. Cardon knocked over one of the Germans and fled by leaping from an upstairs window, but his wife was apprehended with Hull and taken away. Their three children, Marie Jeanne, five, Gustave, four, and two-year-old Gabrielle were abandoned in the home. Gustave Cardon went to the home of his parents in Le Cateau, where a friend of Julie-Celestine saw him towards midnight, bootless and without a coat in the pouring rain. He was half demented and repeating, '*Ma pauvre femme!Mon pauvre ami Herbert!*' (My poor wife! My poor friend Herbert!). Not wanting to implicate his parents, he stayed only briefly, just long enough to tell them what had happened. He also knew that Mme Baudhuin was hiding David and asked that she be warned. He fled to the woods and only a quarter of an hour later his parents' home was searched by four of the many Germans who were clearly closing in on him. He had also managed to send a message to Mme Belmont-Gobert in Bertry who was hiding Trooper Fowler.

Mme Cardon and Hull were taken to Caudry, where they were questioned and physically abused. Hull was particularly badly beaten, and starved, but brave villagers risked themselves to smuggle food to his dark, damp cell. Eight days later at a German tribunal both were sentenced to death. Afterwards they were kept in adjacent cells, and Hull was chained, but a gap in the wall allowed them to talk and Mme Cardon tried to keep his spirits up as they awaited confirmation of their sentences. Hers was reduced to twenty years' hard labour. But Hull had given up hope and could not be consoled; he knew he would die. He became obsessed that his parents should know the truth, so he made Mme Cardon promise that she would tell them. As he was not allowed writing materials he repeated in whispers their address over and over again to the Frenchwoman and she repeated it back. He could not spell it out to her as she did not understand the English letters, but patiently she stuck with it and committed his words to memory. She heard them take Hull away on the night of 21 October 1915 and was choking so much on her tears that she could not call out a final farewell. Her captors told her the next day that he had faced his death bravely.

Mme Cardon was sent to Siegburg prison in Germany. She was to share this fate with a number of friends during her period of incarceration. The Germans would tolerate no opposition in either word or deed and the doctor of Bertry, Dr Charles Eloire, was arrested and deported for three years because of 'observations' he made on Irma Ferlicot. At the end of the war this traitor shared the fate of her victims. She was quickly turned in by her neighbours, arrested by the French authorities, put on trial and sentenced to imprisonment; she died in custody.

The tightening of security in the area following the arrest and execution of Corporal Hull meant that any remote dreams of escape David had left were crushed. Not only had security tightened but a further restriction of the food ration had exacerbated Julie-Celestine's problems in feeding everyone. The Germans were well organized in the management of the occupied region and every person had to be registered and accounted for. They also kept a register of farm animals and food supplies. Rations were allocated to each family according to the number of people registered. Clearly, David was not registered so no allocation of food was made for him; thus simply getting enough for a meagre diet was a daily worry. Close friends and neighbours would help when they could, but there was little to spare.

The situation was the same across the occupied region and was a great problem for Mme Belmont-Gobert and her daughter Angèle, who were still hiding Trooper Patrick Fowler. She had had the idea of concealing Fowler in a large free-standing cupboard in the small living room of her home. It had two doors and contained shelves in one half and hanging space for clothes in the other. By removing the clothes and putting some bedding in the bottom it was possible to hide Fowler inside. It was cramped, but he was able to creep out at night to stretch his legs. In a 1927 interview Angèle explained that their problems were compounded by the fact that twenty-six Germans were billeted with them, but they were determined to protect their fugitive. One of their ploys was to keep the left hand door closed but leave the other ajar, so that their 'guests' could see into the part of the cupboard which contained normal household items without realizing that the other section contained an enemy soldier.

During his long periods in the cupboard Fowler had to remain completely still and silent. Of course he could hear what was going on around him and he knew when the Germans were in the room. On one occasion a neighbour's dog appeared in the room and began sniffing and scratching at the door to his hiding place. Madame quickly chased the animal from the house but the Germans had taken notice of its behaviour and one said, 'Do you have contraband food hidden, Madame? Perhaps we should search it for your hidden treasures.' It was a heart-stopping moment and all seemed lost. But luckily they did not carry out the threat, and Fowler remained undetected.

This was not the only close shave. Angèle recalled:

On another occasion, when the house was empty of Germans, Fowler was out of his *armoire* [cupboard] and in the room with Madame Belmont-Gobert. Suddenly there was a pounding at the door but for some unknown reason Madame pushed her fugitive under the mattress of a heavy timber framed bed instead of into the *armoire*. Seconds later the patrol entered the room and began their search, this time they did open both doors of the *armoire* finding only harmless household items in one side and the crumpled bedding in the other.

Puzzled, one asked, 'Why do you keep this bedding in here Madame?'

She calmly replied, 'Because you Germans have taken over my home and there is nowhere else for me to put it.'

Having searched the room, one soldier pierced the mattress with his bayonet before leaving. Thankfully, it missed the terrified trooper.

Following the tragedy at the Cardon house it was decided that Fowler, too, should be moved for a while. Mme Belmont-Gobert arranged for him to be hidden by friends in a hole below their barn. Fowler was disguised as a woman in order to take the perilous walk from the widow's home to his new hiding place. Angèle recalled that Fowler had a beard and her mother was terrified that this would be spotted during his transfer, but it was a dark and wet night and he was able to pull a shawl close around his head and face, so the journey was completed without incident. For a month he hid in the barn, spending much of his time in the hole beneath it. Food was smuggled in but there was never much to spare, and as a result of his cold and damp living conditions and lack of exercise he fell ill. Thankfully, Bertry too had its heroic pharmacist, named Baudet. Both he and his wife risked their lives tending Fowler during his illness, providing not only medicines but also any food that could be spared. Mme Baudet met Angèle in the cemetery to hand over these clandestine supplies.

Another crisis occurred when Mme Belmont-Gobert was ordered out of her home to make room for even more troops. She was sent to a smaller property a few streets away with only one room and a loft. Despite its small size, Germans were billeted in the loft of this tiny abode which was accessed by an exterior ladder. Luckily they did not requisition her furniture. Her few household belongings would not take long to transport, but moving the cupboard containing Fowler was a tricky problem. There are two accounts of how it was done. The first has Louis Basquin and Fowler moving it at night as the Germans slept. The other is more dramatic. Allegedly, seeing the less than youthful owner and Angèle struggling with the heavy load, two of her German guests volunteered to help carry it to her new home with Fowler inside! If this is true, one can only wonder what the Germans thought was in the cupboard and why they did not take a look.

The move may have added to Madame's worries, but Fowler felt it was a decided improvement, as the new abode was on the edge of the town giving him easy access to the countryside. In a 1927 interview with a reporter from the *Daily Telegraph*, Fowler recalled,

'It suited me better in one way, it was on the outskirts of Bertry and I could get out more easily into the fields.' He was also able to leave his hiding place at night, as he explained: 'When the Germans upstairs had gone to bed I used to hop out of the wardrobe and lie down on a bed screened off with a blanket. The Germans had to come down a ladder to get out of the loft, and as soon as I heard a footstep I would hop back into the wardrobe again, or slip out the back way into the fields.'

Mme Belmont-Gobert and Angèle were keen to provide Patrice, as they called him, with any small comfort they could. He enjoyed a smoke when the *Boches* were out of the way, and one day Angèle noticed a large pipe hanging on a wall in the Germans' upstairs room. This was too tempting, so she stole it for Fowler. How he laughed when she gave it to him, and how he enjoyed his occasional smoke when he could get hold of a pinch of tobacco. Angèle recalled in 1927: 'The *Boches* used to come into our room and sit around the fire making coffee and all the time there was Patrice sitting in the wardrobe. It was so amusing for me to watch them. *Maman* was often afraid but I was young and never afraid.' Angèle revealed that Fowler would sneak out on rare occasions to get some exercise, always during the hours of darkness, accompanied by Louis Basquin; on one of these sorties he paid a visit to Hull at the Cardon home, but the visit was never repeated due to the ever present and increasing fear of capture. Fowler was deeply upset when told of Hull's discovery and death. It was known that Hull's betrayer had told the Germans that another British soldier was being hidden in Bertry, but she could give them no address.

Fowler was now suffering repeated bouts of ill health, but time after time the faithful pharmacist Baudet and his wife came to the rescue with medicines that somehow kept him going. Regularly, Mme Baudet went to the Belmont-Gobert house or to the cemetery to meet Angèle and she knew that she was putting herself and her husband in great danger and understood what their fate would be should they be caught or betrayed. But they knew that they had a duty to do all they could for the stricken soldier.

As time went on, however, the health of Mme Belmont-Gobert also gave way under the strain, and frequently she had what Angèle described as nervous collapses:

One day, *Maman* fell down in the room in one of these attacks. I was out at the time, and Patrice jumped out of the *buffet* and tended her. He was in a terrible state of anxiety when I came in. I took charge of *Maman* and persuaded Patrice to return to the *buffet* and it was well he did so, for a little later some Germans came downstairs to make coffee in the room.

In the latter part of the war both Fowler and Mme Belmont-Gobert were often ill, and it was then that Angèle had more reason than ever to be grateful to the brave Baudets for their sympathy and support in providing medicines and food.

By September 1916 David had been sheltered by the Baudhuin family for over two years, and his outings dressed as a woman, usually accompanied by Aimée, were almost an everyday occurrence and attracted little attention. Perhaps not surprisingly in the circumstances, they had indeed become very close – in fact they were now deeply in love. Still only a few trusted people in the town knew that the young lady known to them as Mademoiselle Louise was a fugitive British soldier. David was by now very confident in his female disguise, but remained very cautious during his outings. Although almost fluent in the local patois, he was careful who he spoke to, never knowing who might be in the pay of the Germans. Herbert Walton writing in the *Daily Telegraph* in 1927 explained that after the first months of his concealment he never had to suffer the experiences of Trooper Fowler or Corporal Hull at Bertry. Once he took up his disguise as a woman he was able to wander through the town almost at will with Aimée or others. He was young and slightly built and it never struck the German patrols that this 'lady' was an enemy soldier.

But someone knew. As was the case in Bertry, Le Cateau, too, had a *Mauvaise Française*, in this case Madame D. She had seen through David's disguise and had spoken to him on occasions when he was dressed up, saying that she knew exactly who and what he was. She made it clear just what would buy her silence. Her advances were rejected by David, but Madame D became ever more insistent and threatening when rebuffed. He would be sorry one day, she said. But while her threats may have at first been empty, things were about to change in dramatic fashion.

Chapter 7

Caught

Although David's active war as a soldier in British army uniform may have ended swiftly at Le Cateau, despite his daily fears and trials as a hideaway in the town, the struggle of his comrades at the front ground on. How much genuine war news he received in his hiding place it is difficult to gauge, but it can only have been little. Rumours were rife but rarely accurate, and news from free France or further afield rarer still. German-produced newspapers were hardly likely to tell the truth, presenting only carefully selected information which put the Germans in the best possible light and showed their enemies making no or merely unimportant and costly territorial gains. The very fact that the Germans were still in occupation of the town and pretty much where they had ended up in 1914 showed the Allies had not made the breakthrough which those occupied and held captive hoped for. David had more than two years in this testing limbo, better than capture certainly but still in constant fear of discovery and betrayal. And as he grew dependent on and fond of his protectors, he no doubt knew they would suffer the harsh penalties threatened by the occupiers if he was discovered.

While the belief for many in Britain had been that it would all be 'over by Christmas', the reality was that David saw the Yuletides of 1914 and 1915 pass without any real evidence that his ordeal would end any time soon. The attempted Allied breakthrough and thrust for victory had not failed for want of trying, but as the trench lines settled and then became fixed, it became obvious that only substantial offensive action would clear the trenches and restore a war of movement. Defences which had started as a provisional means of seeing out the first weeks of war became more and more permanent. Both sides initially shared the illusion of a quick victory, but the Germans were on occupied territory and held the advantage. They could almost win the war by default simply by staying where they were. If the enemy could not break through, victory would be theirs.

Attackers tended to take more losses than defenders hunkered down in trenches with wire and machine-guns and with artillery behind them.

Arguably, it was 1915 which taught this hard lesson to the Germans first. They wanted and needed a quick victory. In April they launched another attack on the northern end of their lines at Ypres, already a killing ground for both sides the previous autumn, and they added a new and terrible weapon – poison chlorine gas. In reality, gas was not a 'new' weapon at all; both sides knew of it and had the capability to make and use it, but it had supposedly been outlawed by an international treaty signed in 1908. Germany decided, however, that it might be just the thing to settle the issue in the west and avoid a prolonged two-front war. The new weapon, wind-delivered from cylinders taken up to the lines, did bring surprise and some initial tactical and territorial gains, but failed to settle the issue. In the absence of masks, defending soldiers urinated onto spare socks or handkerchiefs, which they held over their mouths and noses to counteract the chlorine, and held on. The Second Battle of Ypres saw both sides lose another 50,000 men, and the Allies used the German deployment of gas as further evidence of Hun bestiality and another reason why the war against them had to be pursued.

While hard weather and fatigue, as well as the already tremendous losses, had supposedly halted the war for almost everyone else in the winter of 1914/15, no one seems to have told the French General Staff, who continued with their almost endless efforts in the Champagne area , but with little gain. It was, understandably, a sacred cause for the French to evict the Germans from their soil as soon as possible, and it seemed it was going to have to be accomplished by brute force. Efforts continued almost unabated in Champagne through 1915, and in other parts of the front, particularly Artois further north; but with the Germans still solidly entrenched, this contributed little to ending the war; in fact, it merely saw many more Frenchmen added to the casualty lists. France's strategy of constant attack was already costing her dear. Fuelling this mode of warfare was a school of thought among the French high command that the Napoleonic doctrine of offence was all that mattered and would win the day. Sadly, the Germans also had iron willpower, and much firepower too. The ludicrously visible red trousers as worn by Napoleon's infantry, coupled with such tactics, proved disastrous for the French early in the war. The *pantalons rouges* were quickly ditched for horizon-blue uniforms, but other remedies were not so quickly found.

The British had not been idle either in 1915. Just holding the line tied up a lot of men and supplies, and it was accepted that this would not win the war. The British confidently told themselves that 1914 had been a temporary setback, soon to be remedied. Thus their first offensive of the war was launched that March at Neuve Chapelle, using Indian troops as well as British. Though piercing the German lines initially, it gained little apart from displaying British spirit, especially to the French who in some parts were still a little dubious of their ally's intentions after centuries of rivalry and distrust. Efforts were also made on the nearby Aubers Ridge but with little result. The biggest British effort on the Western Front that year was to support another French Champagne offensive in September. The place chosen was Loos. Supporting the attack theoretically (and making up for a lack of artillery) would be the first British deployment of gas. After the German use of it, the gloves were deemed to be off. Echoing Neuve Chapelle, there were some small gains but no breakthrough, and overall losses were heavy at around 50,000 men. The Cams fought there but took light casualties. The Germans remained masters of the field in the west.

All of this was expected to change in 1916, however, with a plan which would finally breach the German lines, get the war moving again and bring victory. The location chosen was the Somme. Here the British would fight side by side with their French allies, and their efforts would be aided on the bigger stage by offensives from their Russian and Italian allies on other fronts. Two extra factors were now believed to give Britain the edge: her army now numbered a million, and it was backed by a formidable assembly of guns and shells, the like of which had never been seen before. This artillery would open fire before the infantry attack, blasting the enemy into submission. The Germans could not possibly survive its fury. That was the hope and expectation, but the reality was to prove very different.

David would undoubtedly have heard the barrage begin for the Battle of the Somme on 24 June, since Le Cateau is only some 30 miles away as the crow flies. The sound could be heard on the English south coast when the wind blew in from the Continent. With a gun for every fifteen yards of the front and one and a half million shells stockpiled to be fired over a week, it is easy to understand why. Did David finally think that the hour of his deliverance was at hand? For those in the know confidence was high in this offensive, dubbed 'the Big Push'. But the Germans were confident too. They had been on the Somme for two years, had picked all the best defensive positions and fortified their front. They had extensive barbed wire and had been incredibly industrious at digging in the Picardy chalk, much more suitable for the job than Flanders clay. They dug large, deep and dry shelters, offering shell-proof protection for their inhabitants – a key factor in the coming offensive. There were other factors, too: while the British barrage looked good, many shells were of too light a calibre to penetrate the German positions and it is estimated that a third of them failed to explode due to faulty fuses; added to this, inexperienced gunners frequently missed their targets, the very targets which green but keen infantry expected to have been destroyed thereby giving them a walkover.

Any good fortune which may have been around on 1 July, the day the assault opened, seemed to be with the Germans. The French insisted for the most part on an 0730 hrs attack, explaining that daylight would aid visibility, against the British preference for a pre-dawn start covered by darkness. Visibility most certainly did aid the Germans, as wave after wave of British infantry moved steadily towards them on this beautiful sunny morning, presenting a most perfect target which the Germans could not and did not miss. The tactics for the infantry had been kept as simple as possible for most, in the belief that the German defences and their defenders had been flattened by the shelling, which they had not been. As such, the opening day of the Somme became the blackest in the nation's military history, with some 20,000 men killed and another 40,000 wounded, missing and taken prisoner.

David's thoughts must certainly have drifted many times to how his comrades were faring, and perhaps never more so than now as the Somme battle raged. He would not only have heard the barrage but, soon after its opening day, seen many wounded arriving in Le Cateau, which was a major hospital centre. David may have been out of the fight since the end of September 1914, but his battalion had not been, though he knew not where, on which part of the front or in which battles they had been involved. Though not a soldier long, regimental spirit would have been instilled in him and he must have longed for news. Actually, the 1st Cameronians had not really had too tough a war of it compared to some. After retiring from Le Cateau without him, they had continued for almost a month in the general British withdrawal over the Marne and to the Aisne. There had been little real fighting, mostly withdrawal, although there was heavy German shelling of the battalion on the Marne. While they maintained cohesion, it was still extremely disheartening for the troops to be moving away from the enemy.

Following the halting of the Germans at the Aisne, British supply and communication lines were now stretched, so an agreement was made with the French for a British move further north nearer the Channel ports, their natural points for reinforcements. The Cams began their part in this journey on 5 October by rail to St Remy on the Somme, then marched (now forward!) for two days before taking another train to St Omer and moving in stages over the next few days to the Belgian town of Vlamertinghe, just behind Ypres. From here they were bussed back over the border to Laventie, arriving on 19 October. They went into trenches near Fromelles, just in time for the Battle of Armentières, as the Germans tried to round the British and French and make for the coast. In a scenario now familiar to the Cams, no sooner did they arrive than they had to fight and then withdraw. But unlike Le Cateau or indeed anything they had seen so far, this time they took real casualties, losing their first officers, Captain Ronald Rose killed in action and Captain Arthur Ritchie to wounds, on 22 October along with nineteen other ranks listed as killed and thirty-five wounded. Four days later, another officer and thirteen men were killed as well as eleven injured when new lines were established and then held some three miles back. Two weeks later, they moved to trenches around Houplines 10 miles further north with the enemy trenches just 100 yards away, but thankfully quieter. Their year ended not in victory but on rest behind Armentières, famous for its *mademoiselle* of the marching song, though few were in the mood for singing as sixty-four of their comrades and three officers had now been killed since the war started.

The area would remain their home and scene of operations until the autumn of 1915 and their involvement in Loos, which saw the biggest spike in their casualties, though not a steep one compared to other units. September saw thirty-one other ranks killed, and the total for the year was ninety-six men and four officers. Their luck held and this pattern was maintained throughout the first half of 1916, with just one officer and twenty-nine men lost. But when the Somme started the Cams would inevitably get their turn and on 8 July they arrived at Amiens. A week later they were in support trenches near Bazentin-le-Petit, taking four deaths to shelling on their first day there. Much worse was to follow: on 20 July they attacked High Wood and took 382 casualties, including 106 men and four officers killed. It was easily the blackest day of the conflict so far for the unit and remained so for the entire war, despite many hard battles still to be faced. More trench holding, and therefore casualties, took place throughout the summer, mixed with spells out of the line and one final grim flourish towards the battle's end in appalling mud, attacking Hazy Trench near Lesboeufs on 29 October; fifty-nine men were killed and little ground gained. In total, the Somme cost the battalion 230 other ranks killed along with five officers, and perhaps twice as many wounded.

But as grim as the Somme was for the British, and for the French who were fighting alongside their allies despite also contending with the continuing enemy onslaught at Verdun, the Germans were suffering heavily too in 1916. It was also a year of great frustration for them because the aim of their Verdun offensive had been to knock France out of the war by 'bleeding her white' and forcing her to sue for peace, thereby making it difficult for the British to maintain the fight on French soil. But the French were made of sterner stuff and they showed little sign of pulling the plug. Moreover, the losses for the Germans had been just as appalling, with both sides losing around 250,000 men at the aptly-named 'mincer on the Meuse'. And while the blocking of a British breakthrough on the Somme may have brought some sense of achievement to the Germans, the battle was proving to be another huge and sustained one, with their losses ever mounting. By its close, towards the end of November, the Germans had sustained some 600,000 more losses, and victory seemed no nearer.

But even as British High Command was planning victory on the Somme, the ordeal of concealment went on for the stragglers, who could only hope that the expected summer offensive would bring their deliverance. At Villeret, 22 miles from David, Robert Digby and six comrades were living in disguise as peasant villagers and had seemingly blended in well. Digby already spoke decent French, but former Privates William Thorpe, Thomas Donohoe, David Martin, Harry May and Willie O'Sullivan and Corporal John Edwards had also learned a bit of the local patois to fool the Germans. Digby had made at least two attempts to reach his own lines but both had failed and he had returned to Villeret. As 1916 began, however, Digby now had perhaps a strong reason to stay, as he and the village belle, Claire Dessenne, had fallen for each other on sight in August 1914; he was twenty-eight and she just twenty. Claire had been courted by many of the village boys and had dismissed them all, but soon she and Robert became lovers and in November 1915 she gave birth to his daughter, whom they named Helène.

Villeret came under the *Kommandantur* of Le Catelet 5 miles away. Its head was the fanatical Major Evers and he had become increasingly obsessed with the idea that there were still fugitive British soldiers in his area. He ruled the district with an iron rod and soon everyone was suffering from his petty tyrannies, but he stuck with the subject of the stragglers and issued a stream of ever more threatening proclamations. On top of this he set up his own system of intelligence gathering based on collaborators and informers. A combination of fear and a perhaps a dash of jealousy was finally to lead to the men's undoing.

The villagers of Villeret were used to the threats of Evers, but the latest spy scare proclamation posted at the town hall at the end of March 1916 came from the German Army's Commander-in-Chief and it offered a combination of carrot and stick. It declared that hidden soldiers had been found in the area and it was known that there were others; but any straggler giving himself up by the end of April would face no punishment and become an official prisoner of war. After that date it would be imprisonment or death. Harsh penalties would also be imposed on those hiding the soldiers and on the mayor and the whole community. It was a shrewd move by the Germans, instilling fear and playing to those *Mauvais Français* who might be willing to turn betrayer. And it soon worked, because the soldiers – all except Digby – decided for the safety of the entire village to leave; so off they went, only to return two days later saying the area was stiff with Germans. The ever solitary John Edwards did make a solo attempt but was captured 10 miles away. He was sentenced to death but managed to persuade the court he was a Red Cross member not a soldier, so got fifteen years in prison. May and O'Sullivan were also soon caught. Crucially, though, none gave any extra information to the Germans.

Only four now remained in Villeret – Digby, Thorpe, Donohoe and Martin – but the fear among the villagers was palpable as the April deadline approached. An official delegation from the village visited the men and 'strongly advised' them to make another attempt to get away. Money, food and a guide were also offered. So, on 26 April, they set off again, and the villagers held their breath that this time they would succeed and the threat to them all would be lifted. But it was to prove another forlorn hope; two days later the men were all back again saying escape was impossible.

So the men went back to their usual routine; indeed, the deadline passed without any apparent repercussions on the village. But clearly not everyone was happy, and someone was willing to bring matters to a head. On 16 May there was a dawn raid by German military police on the hay loft where the men slept. Digby was quick and managed to escape into the woods, but his three comrades were captured. Several villagers were rounded up too, suspected of having hidden and given support to the men. At a trial four days later fines and prison sentences were handed down to these locals, but the three British soldiers were sentenced to be executed – to be confirmed by a higher court at St Quentin 10 miles away.

Digby remained free, however, and Major Evers made the acting mayor Emile Marié go into the woods to find him with an offer. Marié knew the Englishman well, found his quarry and told him that the *Kommandant* had promised his life would be spared if he gave himself up. He was also told that his friends were to be executed, so he could have been in little doubt that it was only an empty promise. But it was backed by a threat: if he did not come in and surrender there would be harsh punishments meted out to the whole village. As his relationship with Claire and the existence of their baby were widely known, he realized that the people he loved most in the world were now in the gravest danger. He was given the night to think it over, but in reality there was only one decision he could make. As 22 May dawned he gave himself up and he was tried the same day, accused of spying and passing on secrets. He denied both charges but within an hour was found guilty and sentenced to be shot.

All the sentences were confirmed, and on 27 May Thorpe, Donohoe and Martin were executed in front of the chateau walls of Le Catelet where they had been held. Digby saw them taken away and would have heard the volley of shots which killed them. The residents had been ordered to stay indoors but many watched the sad procession pass their windows. Digby suffered the same fate three days later, and all four were buried in the village churchyard. Evers was furious when villagers covered their graves with flowers and ordered them taken away, but he could not prevent a Mass being said for the men. Their graves remain there to this day. A plaque to the men was unveiled on the chateau walls in the late 1990s and the daughter of Robert Digby and Claire Dessenne, Helène, who still lived locally, attended the ceremony. In fact, she lived on into the second decade of the twenty-first century.

It is perhaps therefore not surprising that the latter stages of the Battle of the Somme saw a final end to David's freedom, as the Germans increased the pressure on their occupied zones. They started making ever harsher requisition demands on the already hard pressed locals and issued ever greater threats about the penalties which would follow if anyone was caught helping escaped soldiers. They traded on the fear of retribution against whole communities if soldiers were found in hiding, but also on the baseness of human nature – and it was seemingly this latter motive which did for David. He remained convinced that his betrayer was Madame D, who had seen him cowering for his life on that first day in Le Cateau two years before. David had seemed to pick up the idea, even in the trying circumstances of that first encounter, that he had not seen the last of her. She went on to make it clear afterwards that she remembered him and that the only way for him to buy her silence was to sleep with her. David rebuffed her many times, but each time her threats became more malevolent. He tried to appeal to her better nature by saying that he already had a girl and he did not want to deceive her, but nothing seemed to make a difference. At first, since nothing happened, her threats seemed to be empty and David hoped that it might all be hot air, but she kept on at him and the warnings became ever more threatening. It seems that his good luck was about to run out.

So, just before midnight on 10 September, there was a hammering on the unlocked Baudhuin door and at the same instant four armed German soldiers burst in. The timing had undoubtedly been chosen in the hope that their target would not be hidden but tucked up in bed asleep and unable to flee, and this proved to be the case. The soldiers seemed to know just where to look, too, sending someone up to the loft, which had indeed been a previous hiding place, while others searched downstairs and in the garden. But of chief interest to them was an upstairs bedroom. Julie-Celestine tried to stay calm and would later say:

I prayed very hard and hoped that once more we might escape miraculously as we had already escaped on previous occasions. I was terrified because David was sharing a bed with Léon and we didn't have the time to take him to his old hiding place or put him in the laundry basket.

She did try to act affronted and pointed out she had been searched many times before so there was clearly nothing to find, but the Germans were not to be put off.

One of the Germans went up to the bed in which David and Léon had been asleep – both were now, of course wide awake.
'Who is this?' he asked, pointing to Léon.
'My son Léon.'
How I was trembling. I could scarcely speak.
Léon, too, was shaking like a leaf and it was clear that he not alone in the bed. She continued:
The Boche gave me a malicious, triumphant look, and jerking down the bedclothes revealed David.
'And who is this?'

She desperately tried to explain that he was merely a cousin from the countryside who staying over with them, but this was brushed aside.

Attention now turned fully to David, who initially tried to remain calm and offer a plausible excuse. There were four armed soldiers looming over him with an officer in charge, and he was roughly dragged out of the bed and on to his feet in front of them. He later said:

They shouted at me in French; in the same language I asked them what they wanted with me at such an hour.

'You are English,' cried the commanding officer, incapable of containing his anger.

In the circumstances, David did probably not notice the mistake by the Germans, for he was indeed in all honesty not English! He tried hard to continue the pretence of complete innocence and even tried indignation:

Still in French I calmly and firmly replied to them that I should like them to withdraw from my room and leave me in peace, adding with a hint of impatience, 'This is at least the tenth time you have troubled me with this ridiculous tale.'

The officer was having none of it, though: 'Don't take such pains. You cannot go on with this act any longer.'

Of course we only have David's version of these events and in the telling of his story to journalists in later and calmer times we have already seen that he was more than willing and capable of putting a little extra veneer on things to present himself in a braver and nobler light. One cannot help but feel that perhaps this is exactly what is happening here, as David went on to add that as the officer continued to question him, he got back into bed! He said:

He continued to speak to me in English. I feigned not to understand the language and put my head back on the pillow as if to go back to sleep. Even at his threats to blow my brains out I pretended not to understand what he was talking about. Returning to French, he ordered me to get up, adding that I could give all of the explanations I wished to the *Kommandantur*. Persuaded that it was useless to go on pretending any more, I got up and dressed slowly. At this time the Krauts were unaware of my feminine disguise otherwise they would probably have shot me point blank. After having eaten a little I took a bottle of wine and took a glass of it to steady my nerves, presuming that I would have serious difficulties to endure. I noticed that the Germans were starting to lose patience. I irritated them a little more by gently asking if they were ready to leave. One of them, the sergeant-major, smiled seeing how calmly I was taking the affair.

David was not alone in being arrested; taken away with him by the soldiers were the terrified Léon and Julie-Celestine, who were obviously thought to be in on the subterfuge. Julie-Celestine vociferously and strenuously tried to protest, saying she could not possibly leave the young Marie alone in the house. She said later:

I tried to touch the hearts of the Germans by imploring them not to drag me away from the infant, but my appeals were in vain, and the three of us were marched off to the prison. It was torture to me to imagine what would become of her.

It must have been a deeply traumatizing experience for the fourteen-year-old Marie too, now left frightened and alone in the house. It was lucky that not all in Le Cateau were *mauvais*, and neighbours, despite having so little themselves, rallied around the poor girl to take care of her.

The immediate destination of the arrestees was the nearby former convent on Rue Cuvier. It had been abandoned by the sisters in 1906 due a change in the law on religious education but it remained an imposing building. It was now called the Hotel des Haricots and had been converted into a prison by the Germans; within its dismal walls were locals who had fallen foul of enemy decrees or were even being held hostage as an example to others. Dr Tison was one of the few Le Cateau residents who had frequent access, to treat sick inmates, and he described it as a very dilapidated place which the Germans had done nothing to improve. David was held in a cellar room and certainly did not remember it with any degree of fondness:

It was a depressing stay, but luckily there was a brick missing from the wall; it was the only opening in my cell which let the air through except when the door was opened. In a nearby block were the women and girls who had refused to work for the enemy. For a bed I had a handful of straw and my food consisted of a thin slice of black bread. I started to become feeble and thin like a starving rat. I stayed thus in the black dungeon awaiting the council of war during which my fate would be decided upon.

It must have been a very hard time for him, for as well as the fear and physical hardship, there was the knowledge that the Baudhuin family, who had done so much for him for so long, was now also in great danger and facing a very uncertain future. Just what that future might be it did not take too vivid an imagination to picture, since the Germans had already executed people for much less. David was, ultimately, a soldier out of uniform which itself was against military law. He was also now apart from his beloved Aimée, who had been a great support to him, and he must have worried that her part in the saga would be discovered and she too might be arrested. But he had not been forgotten, and there were still some extremely brave locals who were willing to take great risks for him and the others imprisoned. David explained later:

> Without the goodness of the French ladies who secretly threw me some bread and from time to time passed me a little water through the narrow opening in the wall, I would have died of hunger.

It must have raised his spirits as well as helping him physically.

The tribunal to decide the fate of all was held in the town on 16 October, and David's 'trial' was always going to be the main event. His co-accused were brought into the room first and quickly dealt with. Julie-Celestine was sentenced to ten years in a German prison, while Léon was ordered to be sent away from his home to another part of France to carry out labour for the enemy, cutting down trees to support their war effort. Now came David's turn in the dock, and he has left us with an account of proceedings, recalled in 1922. There were no witnesses for the prosecution as such, only questions from a military panel, and no defence representative. He was going to have to speak up for himself. The accusation was swift and simple.

> I was interrogated and accused of spying. In French I denied the accusation. However, after a few minutes they began to

press me with questions in German, French and English. I inevitably realized that I would compromise myself unless I began to answer honestly.

But even then he realized that 'the truth, the whole truth and nothing but the truth' might possibly not paint him or the others around him in the best light, so he had the presence of mind in the circumstances, if he is to be believed, to be a little selective when it came to giving his testimony.

I admitted then to being a British soldier and explained how I had been separated from my regiment after a bitter battle in the streets. But I energetically claimed never to have left the house in which I had taken refuge after the fighting in Le Cateau.

Perhaps in a sense he might have argued with himself that was telling a little of the truth, because Private David Cruickshank had not been doing much gadding about – it had been the unaccused 'Mademoiselle Louise' who was actually the guilty party. Of course, this was a defence that would hardly have helped his cause if it had been offered.

However, he probably realized that whatever his line of argument, the truth was that the Germans actually had little interest in what he had to say and already had their own agenda, however fairly they might try to portray the proceedings. But he stuck with it:

The officers who made up the tribunal indicated with precision where I had been on certain dates, and despite the accuracy of their information, I judged that my only chance was to completely refute their affirmations. I therefore refused to recognize anything that they cited against me.

His mind must have been in a bewildered whirl wondering what to do next and which tack might be the least damaging and dangerous. Even the slickest of trained legal minds might have struggled in these circumstances, but here was David, little more than a frightened youngster with so much at stake as a consequence of what he might say.

Perhaps in a measure to try and buy a little time and gather his thoughts, he tried silence. He later told the reporter: 'Then I decided to stop answering in the belief that by remaining silent I would lessen the risk of compromising myself.' But whatever he tried, the Germans were not terribly interested and soon lost patience altogether; they made it clear abruptly that he had had his say and it was now time for the delivery of the verdict. There was little deliberation among the panel and it could not have been much of a surprise to anyone in the room, including the defendant, just what that verdict was going to be – and indeed was. David said:

> The commandant of the German district who presided over the council of war decided the death penalty, stating that it was perfectly clear that I was a spy.

Now came the most truly remarkable part of the entire tribunal, and it is recounted here as it was told to the writer of the *Chambers Journal* in 1937. The other accused were still in the room and, on hearing the verdict of death against David, Julie-Celestine could no longer contain herself. While others might understandably have blamed all the woes she and her whole family were now suffering on the young Scot and accepted shooting as the least he deserved, she now risked even further punishment on his behalf – possibly even being executed like him. She would later admit that she saw red on hearing the sentence read out and could not help but immediately shout out to appeal for clemency on David's behalf – something she had not done for herself or her own son Léon.

Initially, the head of the military court seemed completely unmoved by the unusual outburst and went on to say that the penalty for such offences was well known, adding that she could have had little doubt that it would end this way if David was caught. But this simple peasant woman and mother was not finished; even after this rebuke from the court she went on, with deep emotion in her voice:

> Ah, but he was so young. The cruel battlefield has already perhaps robbed me of one of my sons and it seemed to me that God had sent this British boy in his place.

At this point, something in either what she had said or how she had spoken had a visible effect on the presiding officer and his tone became kindlier. He asked her: 'Have you had no news of your son?'

Her answer was in the negative and she added, 'God grant that he is a prisoner like his father.'

This response caused a huddled and whispered conversation among the officers; they asked for some documents to be brought from an adjoining office, these papers were then closely scrutinised and a further hushed discussion took place. What came next for the already emotionally shattered Julie-Celestine must have been truly devastating. Holding one of the documents in his hand, the president of the tribunal said, 'I regret to have to tell you Madame – I deeply regret to have to tell you – that your son was killed ten months ago.'

This awful revelation was greeted with moans and a flood of tears from the bereaved woman; everyone in court was hushed in respect for her tragedy, no doubt as much for the way it had been revealed to her as anything else. But then something incredible happened. Julie-Celestine composed herself, stopped her sobbing as best she could, straightened up and continued her plea for David's life. Still choking back her tears, she said to the man who was holding the youngster's life in his hands, 'He is only a boy. I know now that I have lost my own son. Do not take this one away from me.'

It was an appeal directly from the heart, simple but eloquent and emotional, and the effect on the court was electrifying. The broken Julie-Celestine now clearly thought she had nothing more to lose. In the charged silence that followed, the president's brow was seen to furrow deeply. He was an old soldier himself, a veteran of many actions, and he took some time to reflect on what he had seen and heard. No one could imagine what he was thinking. Did he himself have a son at the front – or perhaps he too had been bereaved by the war? After a while he finally spoke to announce that there would be an adjournment, and the officers left the makeshift courtroom for another chamber and further deliberations. How long this took was not recorded, but on their return it was announced by the same president who had been so moved by Julie-Celestine's words that the death sentence on David Cruickshank had now been commuted to one of ten years in prison. By her devotion, remarkably selfless actions and courage, Julie-Celestine Baudhuin had saved the young soldier's life once again.

Chapter 8

In Captivity

David may have escaped with his life following Julie-Celestine's dramatic and emotional intervention in court, but the excitement and limited freedom of his life as Mademoiselle Louise was a thing of the past and he now faced a potentially long and uncertain future as a guest of the Kaiser in Germany. The tension and daily fear of discovery may have gone, but in Le Cateau he had at least had a degree of freedom, within fairly restricted limits, and real contact with the outside world. He had also had a support network, a substitute family and the love of his sweetheart Aimée. Despite her apparent safety at this time, David could not be sure that her part, too, in his concealment and escapades might not be discovered – perhaps by the same route of betrayal by a jealous or bitter *Mauvaise Française.*

His saviour, Julie-Celestine, had also paid the devastatingly high price of a custodial term for her courage and her devotion to her young foreign charge. She knew that she had saved David's life but also that they would no longer be able to see and support each other. They would not be housed in the same prison to serve their sentences, although they would share the same deprivations and anxieties. For Julie-Celestine the burden must have been heavier, with additional worry about what was going on at home with her young daughter Marie, now without both her parents and her elder brothers.

The cruel fact was that David and Julie-Celestine were not only foreign prisoners held in Germany as a result of the war, but also were going to be considered as the lowest of the low, treated and held as common criminals with none of the limited privileges which were supposed to go along with official 'prisoner of war' status. David may still have been technically serving in the army, but he was captured out of uniform and the Germans no longer considered him a soldier. And while for David, at least, this would eventually change, it was initially to civilian prisons that they were both sent. Their situation will be looked at in this chapter, but it is worth considering first in general terms how conditions for prisoners developed as the war went on.

Germany took an incredible 7 million prisoners during the war and some 2.4 million of these were held in Germany itself. In France's catastrophic first few months of war she lost tens of thousands of troops captured by the enemy, and while fewer British were taken prisoner, their number was still substantial. Then there was the vast number of Russians taken on the Eastern Front. Of course, everyone was expecting a short and victorious war, so no proper provision had been made for the masses of men who now needed shelter, food and looking after. The first winter of the war was a very cruel one for POWs, who were often without proper accommodation.

In 1915, the Germans set about a programme of building proper camps for prisoners and these would eventually number around three hundred. Indeed, the Germans were legally bound to care properly for their charges since they had, as recently as 1907, signed the Hague Convention, which laid down the following guidance:

> Prisoners of War are in the hands of the hostile government, but not of the individuals or corps who capture them. They must be humanely treated. All their personal belongings, except arms, horses and military papers, remain their property.

This was the rule as set in an ideal world, but the world at war had a very different reality, whatever reputation the Germans may have had as sticklers for the rules.

Arguably, David and Julie-Celestine were lucky to be captured as late as they were, because it meant that they missed the terrible early days of confusion when the system groaned under the strain. By mid-1916 there were 1.6 million POWs in their country and the Germans had devoted considerable resources to the matter despite still being engaged in a gruelling war on two fronts. But David and Julie-Celestine's initial good fortune would prove illusory as prisoner numbers continued to swell and Germany's ability to care for them was hit not only by the strain of war but by the biting Allied naval blockade, which prevented supplies coming in from overseas.

A typical other ranks POW camp – officers and men were not housed together – with the usual compound German name, *Mannschlaftslager*, saw the men kept in tarred wooden huts measuring 10 metres by 50, with space for 250 occupants. One solitary fire would serve as the hut's somewhat inadequate heat source – if there was any fuel to put in it, since shortages soon started to bite. The huts lacked any real comfort bar their rows of bunk-type beds with mattresses stuffed with dry grass. There was a separate sanitary block, and the authorities tried to keep men clean since disease could be rife in the crowded conditions. Spiritual and cultural needs could sometimes be taken care of in other buildings. Prized, if it existed, was the *Kantine,* where POWs, if they had the funds, were allowed to buy extra supplies of food and writing materials.

Food was always an issue in the camps. Even the simply ritualistic element of meals was important in institutions which lacked freedom and kept men cooped up together. The Hague Convention said that food should be issued at the same level as rations in the captor army, but this soon proved unfeasible. The rules might stress that meat be served three days a week and fish twice, along with daily vegetables and bread; but the reality was that soup soon became the norm, and its contents were often dubious. Real bread gave way to the notorious so-called KK (*Kleie und Kartoffeln*) bread, which was made from a mixture of bran, potato flour, ox blood and even sawdust. Any solid food which might show up, especially meat, was often rotten and likely to make the men ill.

It must be said that, due to the blockade, food was in reality little better for German civilians; the best of what little was available was going to the armed forces. The POWs at least had the opportunity of receiving packages from home which could often contain food. This could and did lead to resentment from the guards, with pernickety searches of packages and sometimes the deliberate spoiling of foodstuffs sent in this way. The famous Red Cross parcels were also sent; but, while extremely welcome, in reality these often contained little more than biscuits. Britain also had a charity, the Central Prisoner of War Committee, which supplied POWs, and the sheer scale of their effort was stupendous: by the end of the war nine million food and 800,000 clothing packages had been sent from

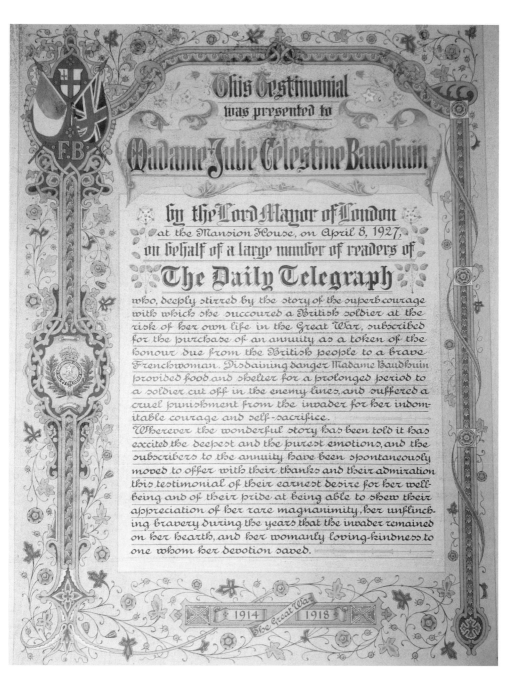

This Testimonial

was presented to

Madame Julie Celestine Baudhuin

by the Lord Mayor of London

at the Mansion House, on April 8, 1927,

on behalf of a large number of readers of

The Daily Telegraph

who, deeply stirred by the story of the superb courage with which she succoured a British soldier at the risk of her own life in the Great War, subscribed for the purchase of an annuity as a token of the honour due from the British people to a brave Frenchwoman. Disdaining danger Madame Baudhuin provided food and shelter for a prolonged period to a soldier cut off in the enemy lines, and suffered a cruel punishment from the invader for her indomitable courage and self-sacrifice.

Wherever the wonderful story has been told it has excited the deepest and the purest emotions, and the subscribers to the annuity have been spontaneously moved to offer with their thanks and their admiration this testimonial of their earnest desire for her well-being and of their pride at being able to shew their appreciation of her rare magnanimity, her unflinching bravery during the years that the invader remained on her hearth, and her womanly loving-kindness to one whom her devotion saved.

1914   The Great War   1918

Testimonial found at the brocante in Etaples. (Author's collection)

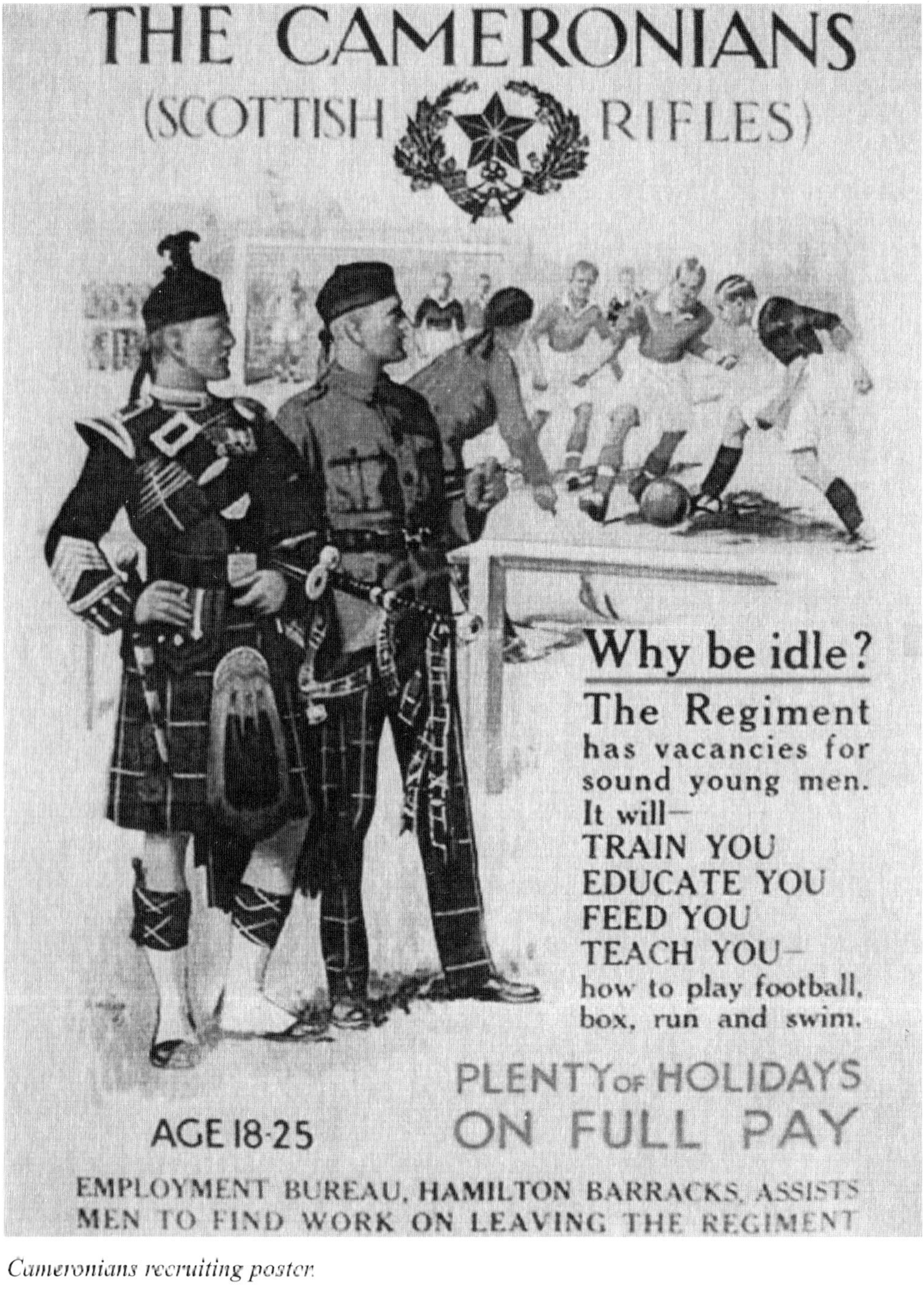

Cameronians recruiting poster.

David Cruickshank in POW uniform. (Glen Cruickshank)

Mme Julie-Celestine Baudhuin, 1920s.

Mme Belmont-Gobert.   *Marie-Louise Cardon.*   *Mme Angèle Lesur.*

Le Cateau railway station before the War. (Author's collection)

Libr. D. Prudhommeaux — Cl. B. F.

6 — **Le Cateau** *(Nord) - La Gare*

War damage in Le Cateau. (Author's collection)

War damage to the church, Le Cateau. (Author's collection)

Le Cateau during the
German occupation –
note the sentry box.
(Author's collection)

A German shop in Le
Cateau. (Le Cateau
archives)

German soldiers in Le Cateau's market place. (Author's collection)

German soldiers posing in Le Cateau. (Author's collection)

Notice issued by Major Haertel announcing the execution of M and Mme Gosse for possession of carrier pigeons and warning that anyone found in possession of carrier pigeons or weapons will be shot without trial. (Le Cateau archives)

AVIS

Je fais savoir par la présente que j'ai du faire fusiller, d'après les lois de la Guerre, le 24 Novembre à 3 heures de l'après-midi, les

Joseph-Cyrille GOSSE et sa femme
Clémence GOSSE

de Catillon, parce qu'ils avaient sciemment contrevenu à l'ordre que j'avais donné d'avoir, sous peine de mort, à remettre à la Commandantur les pigeons-voyageurs.

Les habitants sont, sommés par la présente, pour la dernière fois, d'avoir à remettre à la Commandantur jusqu'au 26 Novembre à 1 heure tous les pigeons-voyageurs, armes et munitions existant encore.

Si cette remise est faite de suite et de bon gré les personnes en question ne seront frappées que d'une amende dont la Commune sera responsable.

Celui qui ne se soumettra pas à cette injonction sera fusillé sans autre formalité.

Si, après ce délai, on trouvait encore des pigeons-voyageurs, armes ou munitions dont les propriétaires sont absents ou inconnus, tous les habitants de la maison où ils seront trouvés en seront rendus responsables. Le maire et toute la commune auront à répondre des maisons inhabitées.

HAERTEL,
Commandant.

The chateau at Guise. (Author's collection)

58 GUISE — Vue intérieure du Château Fort, Puits et Caserne

Aimée Olivier.
(Glen Cruickshank)

David's mother, David, Aimée in Glasgow, 1919. (Glen Cruickshank)

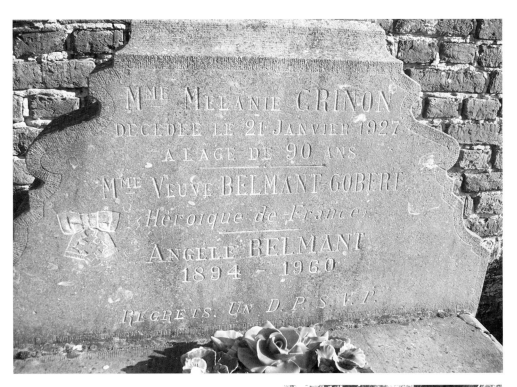

The grave of Mme Belmont-Gobert and Angèle.

Memorial to civilian victims of the War, Le Cateau.

The house in which Mme Belmont-Gobert hid Trooper Fowler.

The Baudhuin home, where the garages are today, was destroyed in 1918.

Le Cateau's covered market, showing war damage. (Author's collection)

The covered market today.

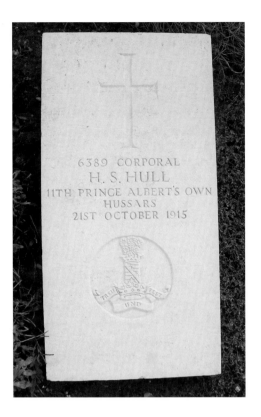

Herbert Hull's headstone.

The house in which the Cardons hid Hull.

Programme of music played at the reception for the French heroines.

PROGRAMME OF MUSIC

BY THE STRING BAND OF THE

Honourable Artillery Company

(By kind permission of the Colonel-Commandant the Earl of Denbigh, C.V.O., A.D.C., T.D., and Court of Assistants).

1.	MARCH	Le Pere la Victoire	*Ganne*
2.	CHANSON	Quand Madelon	*Robert*
3.	SELECTION	Tommies' Tunes, 1914—1918	*Pether*
4.	MARCH	Sambre et Meuse	*Turlèt*
5.	SELECTION	The Rose	*Myddleton*
6.	FOX TROT	Picardy	*Alrose*
7.	SELECTION	Sunny	*Kern*
8.	CHANSON	(A) Hé Marie !	*Chantrier*
		(B) La Marche des Bananes	*Scotto*
		La Marseillaise	*Alrose*
		God Save the King	*Turlèt*

Director of Music - - - - F. GIBBS, *Bandmaster.*

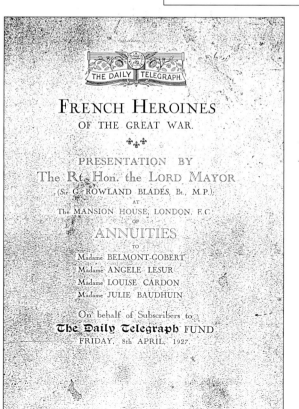

THE DAILY TELEGRAPH

FRENCH HEROINES
OF THE GREAT WAR.

❖❖❖

PRESENTATION BY

The Rt. Hon. the LORD MAYOR

(Sir G. ROWLAND BLADES, Bt., M.P.).

AT

The MANSION HOUSE, LONDON, E.C.

OF

ANNUITIES

TO

Madame BELMONT-GOBERT
Madame ANGELE LESUR
Madame LOUISE CARDON
Madame JULIE BAUDHUIN

On behalf of Subscribers to

The Daily Telegraph FUND

FRIDAY, 8th APRIL, 1927.

Front cover of the programme for the reception of the French heroines.

David and Aimée Cruikshank, 1960s (Glen Cruickshank)

Britain. The Red Cross, set up in 1863 and recognized under the Hague Convention, had sent 16 million parcels by the end of 1915 alone, and it operated 2,000 railway wagons. The Red Cross was also allowed access to the POW camps to make sure that conditions were acceptable – this often led, just prior to visits, to improvements which would last only for the duration of the inspection. Another vital role played by the Red Cross was to assist relatives searching for missing soldiers. It operated the International Prisoner of War Agency, based in Geneva, to which all belligerents were duty bound to supply lists of captives, and it dealt with an average of 16,500 letters a day during the war. This would have been one of the methods desperate families like the Cruikshanks used to search for news of their loved ones after they had been reported missing.

Just as welcome as parcels to the men was word from home in the form of letters and postcards. There was no limit as to how much mail could be received, but writing back was controlled and each man was allowed to write only two letters of four sheets a month and four postcards. The post, of course, was monitored and censored, but great efforts went into devising codes which would be missed by the censors and understood by the letters' recipients. The paper was not automatically supplied and had to be bought from the camp store. Men starved of news devoured any information from home. Rumours were rife and eagerly absorbed by bored men, and the guards would play their part by starting stories which they knew would lower the morale of their captives. Newspapers from home were much sought after but not easily obtained and not officially sanctioned. But the Germans were aware that people tend to believe what they see in a paper, any paper if there is no choice, and so went to a great deal of trouble to produce their own. They came up with *The Continental Times*, which by 1916 had a 15,000 circulation in English and, earlier, in French, the *Gazette des Ardennes*. These organs' declaration that they would tell no lies was, of course, itself a lie; their aim was to undermine morale. As much as they were hated by the captive population behind the lines, they were widely read in the absence of anything else.

Prisoners were always under surveillance and the camps were fenced with thick and high barbed wire. In the early days of the war it had been common for inmates to be paraded in nearby towns to encourage the local population and discourage the prisoners. They were often met with jeers and sometimes violence. Visits were also sometimes made to the camps. But as the conflict lengthened these became fewer, and everyone just settled in for the long haul as fellow sufferers of the war. Camp staffs would usually be headed by unfit or wounded officers, while the guards might be elderly *Landsturm* (militia) members, family men just pressed into service against their will. While petty tyrannies were frequently exercised against their charges, there were often acts of indulgence and kindness too.

Other ranks, unlike officers, could be worked – as long as the work did not aid the war effort, though this was a very blurred line. It did, however, allow for some interaction between prisoners and civilians. With so many men away at the war, Germany certainly needed the muscle of the POWs, and some 1.4 million of them were put to work, with 750,000 working in agriculture and 350,000 in industry. For those on the land it often meant better food and conditions in the fresh air. But the days were long and quotas were not uncommon, with punishments for failures to meet them. Men might actually live off-camp while working, and the surveillance could be slacker. A former POW known to one of the authors in his native Nottinghamshire had been a coal miner before 1914 and was put to work in the German pits after capture on the Somme in 1916. He said that though worked hard he had been treated fairly, and he was overwhelmed by the superior working conditions in the German mines – not equalled back home, he said, until nationalization of the coal industry after the Second World War!

In post-war interviews with the press David was to paint a grim picture of his incarceration in Germany, nor he did paint the brightest picture of his captors. There is no way now of verifying what his treatment at their hands was like, but it must be said that previous tales he had told to the media did not always completely hold water and he seemed to like to play to the gallery to some degree – not forgetting, of course, that he had an axe to grind. Men who had hidden for so long before capture were often singled out for harsh treatment by guards who felt they deserved what they got, having got out of uniform, evaded their duty and escaped the war that others were fighting. In their eyes he was no longer a soldier as he had forfeited that status when he changed out of his uniform and became little more than a foreign criminal. These things must all be borne in mind when considering the account which follows:

From Le Cateau I was taken with brutal treatment to Aix-la-Chapelle (no doubt called Aachen by the Germans!). The slightest movements on my part were taken to be acts of rebellion and served as a pretext to increase the cruel treatment. During my stay in Aix, I was locked into a four-foot-wide metal cage; I had to crouch like a beast in captivity. From time to time a gaoler came to look at me out of the corner of his eye and, by his taunts, attempted to irritate me. Despite the exiguity and hardness of my prison, I was far from being disposed to submission. In the space of ten weeks I lost seven kilos thanks to the exaggerated starvation diet. The Krauts must have agreed between themselves to turn me into a champion of starvation.

From Aix-la-Chapelle they transported me to Cologne (in German – Köln) in an ordinary prisoner wagon. But in this city the same deprivations in terms of food awaited me. What I am about to say will seem unbelievable for those who live comfortably at home; it is none the less true that one day I ate a piece of my handkerchief to appease the gnawing pain in my famished stomach. Other times, I tore the edge of my shirt in order to fulfil the need I had of having something in my mouth. I would have literally starved had it not been for the fact that my bed was made up of dried herbs, most of which I devoured and in very little time so as to ease my hunger. All of this, it can be conceived, caused me intolerable suffering. But could I hope for better days?

From Cologne they took me to Kassel to a huge establishment filled with convicts and which reminded me of Dartmoor. There they put me with the assassins, thieves and delinquents of all kinds, in a word the worst subjects of Germany. In this great prison there were about 600 cells. The Krauts forced me to make cardboard boxes or shoes for their campaigning armies. But I was firmly decided not to bring any assistance to the enemies of my country and I refused to do the work to which they had assigned me. To punish me, they threw me into a dark cell where they tied my hands and neck with a chain weighing forty-five kilos. The Krauts had sworn to break my resistance, but I was resolved not to give in. I slept in my handcuffs. Twice a day my guard came to free one of my hands so that I could eat the small crust of bread which made up my daily ration.

These ill-treatments endured until 1917 ended up making me ill and for two and a half months I had to remain lying on my bed of straw. I began to no longer have the strength to move and often I wished that death would come and put an end to my suffering. At other times, I began to hope again, bourn [*sic*] up by the perspective that a happy event might occur and I would be delivered. One day I asked to see the prison doctor. Since I no longer had the strength to walk, they had to carry me to his surgery. At that time my weight had dropped to fifty-three and a half kilos, whereas it used normally to be seventy-five kilos.

I would have died of starvation when good news arrived. The government was threatening to take reprisals against German prisoners of war if the German government did not allow foodstuffs to be sent to British prisoners held captive in Germany. Food was therefore sent by my regiment: it was my salvation as well as that of a great many other British soldiers.

I had almost lost my sight as a result of my reclusion between four whitewashed walls and I could no longer even read large print letters whereas my eyesight had previously been excellent. Despite my repulsion at the idea of working for the Krauts I realized that I was exposing myself to the risk of blindness if I didn't have other colours to look at than these white walls and I asked to do some woodwork. The job I was given was not very comforting: I had to make coffins for dead prisoners. There was nothing luxurious about this work. The coffins were made of rough planks nailed together. I stayed attached to this task and continued as well as can be expected to put up with the nasty harassment which characterises the Germans.

Back into our story at about this time comes Lieutenant Colonel Crofton Bury Vandeleur DSO, who was introduced in Chapter 4; he, or rather his wife, was to play a very important role in David's life. Two more different men than David and Vandeleur it would have been hard to find; it was only the army that they had in common, but this link would prove crucial in perhaps seeing David through some of his darkest days in captivity. Vandeleur was a career soldier who loved every minute of army life and excelled as a dedicated officer. But before the war, and just as importantly to this story, he had spent many of his early years in Germany where he had been educated in German, and he now spoke it fluently. He married in 1903 and soon fathered a son (later with a distinguished military career himself as a Brigade Commander at Arnhem in 1944 and portrayed by Michael Caine in the film *A Bridge Too Far*!). From 1911, Maryhill in Glasgow had been the family's home, a short distance from the barracks which was now the base of the 1st Cams, with whom Vandeleur was serving.

Major (as he then was) Vandeleur saw action from the start of the war, and by the end of September 1914 three members of his extended family had been killed. By the following month he had been promoted in recognition of his abilities and because of the sheer number of senior officers who had already been lost; he was now the officer in command of the 2nd Cheshires and he was on his way to join them when at La Bassée the unit, weary from its losses, was completely surrounded and he was wounded and taken prisoner by cavalry of the Prussian Guard. Such was the confusion of battle that he was initially reported as missing – something else he would share with David.

Initially, his Prussian captors treated him well and he was given food and shelter. Being a senior officer who spoke fluent German perhaps helped, for he noticed that this treatment was not the norm for all prisoners. He was soon pressed for details about the British Army's dispositions, but his skill in the language was useful in telling his captors in no uncertain terms that they were going to get nothing of use from him. This brought a swift change in demeanour from the Germans, who soon afterwards bundled him on to a train with other POWs headed across northern France towards the Belgian border, en route for Germany. This trained observer paid attention to everything, noting how at Douai they were all forced off the train and into the town's main square, where they were subjected to abuse from

German soldiers. Vandeleur himself was spat at and had his coat taken. He later reported: 'This treatment was deliberately arranged for by a superior authority with the object of making us as miserable as possible.'

Once in Germany itself, he was placed in captivity at a POW camp at Krefeld, close to the border with the Netherlands, where his treatment did improve. The location of the camp, Vandeleur's knowledge of German and his determination to get the better of his captors soon saw him evade them and make it over the border into neutral Holland, from where he became the first British officer to make a successful escape home. The furious Germans took their revenge on those left behind by illegally withdrawing their tobacco ration for a period. Just before Christmas, Vandeleur's son got off the train from his boarding school and was surprised but delighted to be greeted by his father, unusually attired in a stolen German overcoat and a Dutch hat. A very happy festive period no doubt followed for Vandeleur, with a younger brother also back from the front and recovering from wounds.

The British authorities were very interested in anything Colonel Vandeleur could tell them and asked him to submit a report, which he duly did, and which was scathing of his treatment at the hands of the Germans. It ended up on the desk of the Foreign Secretary, Sir Edward Grey, who was so outraged that he had it passed via the neutral Americans in their London Embassy to the Germans in Berlin. The British undoubtedly saw some propaganda value here, but there was also genuine concern over the possible mistreatment of prisoners. The Germans responded with a lengthy rebuttal, which dismissed all Vandeleur's claims and added much abuse. An audience with the King was also arranged for the Colonel to state his case and indirectly have a dig at his sovereign's cousin, the German Emperor Wilhelm II. King George V did not need any encouragement to think the worst of Cousin Willy, who had always been regarded within the royal household as rather full of himself and a bully.

By May 1915 Vandeleur was back on the Western Front, but again his active war was not destined to be a long one. He went over the top with his men at Festubert on 9 May and in this forlorn attack was severely wounded by machine gun fire in no-man's-land in front of the German trenches. Initially, it was thought that he had been captured again, but luckily he was eventually brought back to his own lines. If he had been captured, it would have been interesting to see what treatment he got from the Germans in the light of his previous escapades and his report on them! But it was the end of his fighting war and he spent much of the rest of it in hospital, before commanding a home depot in Scotland, going on half pay in 1919 and retiring after thirty-five years' service in 1922. A legacy of his wound remained crippling arthritis. He died in July 1947.

David, of course, would have been unaware of all this, but he was still a member of the Cameronian regimental family, even if he had occasionally taken to wearing a wig and skirt. The Colonel's wife, Mrs Evelyn Mary Vandeleur, had been very active in instigating a comforts fund for men of the Cams who were now imprisoned by the Germans, and from its inception in June 1915 it had been well supported and provisioned, despite the hardships of the home front. Working with the relevant authorities and the Red Cross, it was soon providing supplies to soldiers caught overseas. Only in late 1916, when David had been officially reported as captured by the Germans, did he come to the attention of the authorities, but they took up his case as one of their own and he was soon added to the list of recipients. As rations were becoming poorer and poorer all the time in Germany, and as David was regarded more as a common criminal than an official POW with Red Cross entitlements, this link could very well have been the difference between his surviving and going under.

It may also have been at this time that David was moved from his civilian prison to be put on a more 'official' footing in a POW camp. Certainly a postcard bearing a photo of him was sent home to Glasgow. He gives his new address as 16th Comp, 1 Camp, No 4 Barrack A, Cottbus, but infuriatingly the year of the postmark is not clear. He is standing in front of a painted backdrop, wearing the strangest array of bits of uniform and is without a cap. Often the camp *Kantine* would provide postcards like this for prisoners. The service was not free, and the mere fact that David could now pay for something like this shows that his conditions had vastly improved. It must have seemed like a miracle to his family back in Scotland, as he would have been given up for dead while in hiding in Le Cateau. Harry Beaumont's wife said she had been informed by the authorities after six months that her husband was officially dead and she then started to receive a widow's pension.

David now also had the chance to mix with his own people and use his own language again. One soldier who met him in 1918 at Soltau was Private Richard Webb of the 4th Dragoon Guards. They must have had a lot to talk about as they had similar experiences of being cut off from their units and then long concealment from the Germans before capture and imprisonment. Webb's story is one of those held at Kew's National Archives. After the war a team of interviewers recorded the stories of about 3,000 men who had been captured. Sadly, David appears not to have been one of those interviewed.

Webb, from Birmingham, was cut off with an NCO, Corporal Cheesman, near Cugny, 20 miles south of St Quentin, on 29 August 1914. After several attempts to rejoin their unit they realized it was hopeless and hid in woods nearby. They were befriended by a local farmer, Emile Fontaine, who brought them food. In December the Germans systematically beat the wood and flushed them out, but they evaded capture and M Fontaine took them to his farm, where he built a pit under a barn for them in which they stayed until August 1915, when they moved to a loft above the barn for a further fourteen months. The winter of 1916 was so cold that the generous Frenchman gave them his own bedroom. In all this time they saw only the farmer and his wife.

On 10 February 1917 the Germans cleared the area and the men had to return to the woods, surviving on food given them by the Fontaines; but on returning to the farm for more supplies they were spotted by a patrol and caught. Weak and bedraggled, they initially pretended to be French soldiers but questioned at Cugny then said they were Irishmen, as the belief was they would therefore be treated better. They had their photos taken by the Germans and were then sent to St Quentin prison. The next day they were interrogated by a German officer with perfect English who seemed to know more about the British Army than they did and refuted their Irish status as, he said, he was Irish himself! He also told them they would be court-martialled.

The court martial took place at Avesnes on 24 February when they were charged with spying and sentenced to death. However, they had an officer speaking for them who protested at the ruling, and ten days later at another hearing they received instead fifteen years in prison for hiding in an occupied country and failing to surrender. Fontaine had been caught, too, and at the same trial he was given ten years. They were initially held locally until 8 April and then sent to Germany, first to a civilian prison in Aachen and then a series of German camps, meeting David Cruickshank in the Königsberg camp at Soltau in January 1918, before David was sent to another prison, which he believed to be Kassel.

The price for helping David had been paid not only by Julie-Celestine but by the entire Baudhuin family. She might have been sentenced to ten years in prison in Germany but her teenage son Léon was also found culpable, was moved away from home and forced to work cutting trees for the Germans. With her father also a captive of the enemy as a prisoner of war, Marie, who was only fourteen, was thus alone in the family house, but the Germans took absolutely no consideration of her plight at all. The extended family and neighbours all rallied round to do what they could, but conditions were hard for everyone and there was little to spare. Even their old house was destroyed later in the war by shelling. Marie did live to see the return of both her parents, but those two terrible years alone blighted her life for long afterwards and she needed regular medical treatment for many years to regain some kind of normal existence.

Julie-Celestine initially followed the same route as David to Cologne, where she was eventually imprisoned in the notorious Siegburg prison. That conditions were tough almost goes without saying, for the women inmates were considered the lowest criminals by their female German guards and little consideration or kindness was given to them. Julie-Celestine remained generally tight-lipped and miserly with detail when asked by journalists after the war about her experiences in captivity. She talked of hard work, bitter cold, lack of food and harsh treatment by the guards, having lost five teeth to a blow from one wardress. 'I was beaten several times. The horror of that life is sometimes with me today as though I was actually undergoing it all again,' she would tell one reporter from *Chambers Journal* as late as 1937. As such, it is perhaps unsurprising that she did not want the memories of those terrible days brought to the surface too often.

Coupled to the sheer physical strain of surviving in such conditions there was undoubtedly the stress of worrying about what she had left behind and what was becoming of Léon and Marie. She would not have been human if she did not torture herself with the question of her responsibility for bringing all this misery and hardship onto herself and her family by her own actions. It was all too late to change anything now. Against this, however, was the consolation offered by the company of fellow inmates and the unity they enjoyed in their defiance of the invader. Indeed, Julie-Celestine had at times in Siegburg the companionship of other women from around the Le Cateau area: Mme Marie-Louise Cardon, who had hidden Corporal Herbert Hull, along with Mme Germaine Chalandre and Mme Léonie Logez.

While Julie-Celestine recorded little about her sufferings at Siegburg, another inmate has left a very detailed account and from this we can gather just how grim the life of the prisoners was. The writer may have shared Julie-Celestine's experiences, but she came from a very different background. Princesse Marie de Croy belonged to an ancient noble family which went back centuries; although centred in Belgium, the family had spread and intermarried to give it branches in France, Austria, Holland, Spain, Russia and even Germany. Many of her ancestors had been warriors or clerics – interestingly, given their roles in the Great War, two had been Bishops of Ypres and Arras. Fluent in many languages as a result of this cosmopolitan background and with a strong sense of Christian and moral duty, her name was widely respected and carried considerable clout.

Princesse Marie was born in 1875 and her home in 1914 was on the family estate near Mons in Belgium. During the battle which bore its name, in the first weeks of the war, Princesse Marie tended many British soldiers and helped a number escape. She also cared for wounded German officers, which may have been the reason why she was initially left alone by the new occupiers of her country. But Princesse Marie considered herself a Belgian patriot; she wanted the Germans out of her country and saw the best way of achieving this as supporting the Allies in the only realistic way possible to her. And so she became a spy. She was perhaps better placed than most due to her noble background which, in those more deferential times, did mean a lot and made access to many places considerably easier. She had been educated in English and spoke German too, as well as having great natural intelligence and courage.

But her luck ran out and in 1915 she was arrested by the Germans and put on trial; noble or not, she was put before a tribunal and sentenced to ten years in prison. So in November she found herself making the journey Julie-Celestine would undertake a year later, to Siegburg prison. She would spend three hard years there but survive to write her war memoirs in 1932. She shared all the trials and tribulations of the other inmates, indeed she refused any favourable treatment which her social position might have brought her, insisting on prison garb when it was suggested she might retain her own clothes. She remained a constant thorn in the side of her German guards and their superiors and refused to allow them to grind her down, breaking the petty rules when possible, devising a code in letters to get and spread news and keeping up the morale of her fellow captives. Indeed, although one might think that her previous life of privilege and comfort would have counted against her in these conditions, if anything it seems to have given her the inner strength to see it through.

Her arrival at Siegburg in the winter of 1915 was dispiriting. She described the prison as drab and cold and she was first taken to a cell in the hospital wing for a medical assessment. What little heating there was came from a single metal pipe which ran through all the cells; it was completely inadequate and turned off anyway at weekends. She said the winter temperature was 9° Centigrade (41° Fahrenheit), but she at least found it bearable if she kept still. Others suffered horribly and, she said, their cries could be heard right through the night. Siegburg had been a prison before the war and still held a good number of civilian prisoners and some very tough characters, murderers included, but these were eventually moved elsewhere.

This was how the daily routine started in the prison according to the Princesse: a bell was sounded, then a warder with two prisoners came round unlocking all the cell doors; toilet pails were emptied and then everyone was locked in again. There were no toilets other than this in the prison, and the ritual was repeated later in the day. All the waste went into a large tin container and, the Princesse said, the smell was extremely unpleasant and got worse when dysentery became common among the prisoners.

There was nothing to eat for breakfast, just coffee, which was extremely weak and without milk or sugar but at least gave some warmth back to the body. No solid food was provided until midday, and then it hardly qualified as such, being just a watery soup. In 1915 a sticky slice of bitter bread was also given, but this became smaller and smaller as the war went on and deteriorated even further in quality. Initially, too, there was meat or fish in the soup but this became rarer, with beetroot or swede becoming the norm, unpeeled and with stem and leaves attached. Most hated was a brown powdery soup of alleged vegetable scrapings dubbed *soupe à la souris* (mouse soup) by the prisoners. This was so disgusting that when it was mixed with other food remnants for local farmers to feed to their pigs, they asked that it be left out as even the animals refused it.

As food quality and quantity dropped, so did inmate morale, and the long and freezing winter of 1916/17 experienced by Julie-Celestine and her fellow prisoners in Siegburg was a terrible one. Princesse Marie wrote of it:

> The snow lay on the ground for weeks together, food got so scarce and so bad in quality that hunger became chronic. Very few understand the real meaning of the word hunger. Most people imagine they are hungry when they have merely acquired a good appetite for the next meal. But the chronic hunger which reigned at this period in Germany had nothing in common with that sensation. A feeling of exhaustion, of irritation, accompanied by violent headache and nausea, persisted night and day, often making sleep impossible.

Indeed, the Princesse well remembered the tortured cries of an elderly woman in a nearby cell which rose in volume and intensity due to her desperate hunger throughout the long and cold nights.

Inmates with wealthier families on the outside might receive parcels containing food. Initially, these were unlimited in size and number, but eventually the Germans reduced the ration to two 5-kilogram packages a month. Anything extra would theoretically be sent back, but understandably perhaps, given the hardships the guards themselves were suffering, there came into existence a burgeoning black market trade in goods filched from these parcels. Nothing of the hardships in prison, especially shortages of food, could be mentioned in letters home. Every second Sunday a sheet of paper or postcard would be distributed along with a pen and ink for writing such missives. Letters from the outside world would be sporadic, frequently out of sequence and with some clearly missing, sometimes smelling of vile chemicals, always opened and censored, but always nonetheless welcome. The Princesse's account offers a snapshot of her own background and of how difficult it was for outsiders to understand the conditions and life endured inside the prison walls – and how frustrating this was for prisoners. One old English friend, who had been her nanny, wrote saying that she hoped that her apartment in the prison was a comfortable one and even wondered whether she might be allowed to come and act as her maid!

Prisoners were exercised in the courtyard outside for half an hour, four paces apart and with strictly no talking allowed. The only concession to the cold was to be told to walk at a brisker pace. Those older or weaker exercised in a less exposed inner courtyard. The no talking rule was strictly enforced even during the acts of worship which took place on Sundays. The working day consisted of weaving, sewing or button-making on huge manual presses, though there was also some harder outside work on the land away from the prison – during which some women managed an escape to Holland and duly sent the prison director a postcard celebrating their arrival. Any misdemeanours were severely punished, and most dreaded was the *cachot*, a tiny cell with a wooden bed and bread-and-water rations. The Princesse said that several women lost all reason when held there, and it seemed to affect most severely those with the simplest or most nervous of natures.

Women, of course, fell ill, and there was a doctor and hospital wing in the prison, but deaths were still not uncommon. The Princesse noted the arbitrary nature of the 'care' of the sick in Siegburg: those who reported sick had to stand in a corridor facing the wall, two paces apart and in silence, until they were called into the doctor's office. There was often only a brief interview before they were rapidly ejected with the word *'Sortez!'* (Get out) ringing in their ears. With grim humour, the medic was known throughout the prison as 'Dr Sortez'. She added that he was clearly under pressure not to prescribe medicines, which were undoubtedly in as short supply as everything else, and he would only do so, or order an improved diet, in the severest cases. Most prisoners were aware of this and many did not even bother reporting sick no matter how ill they felt. The Princesse recalled at least one prisoner who was found dead in bed at unlocking time in the morning. At the other end of life, there were also births in the prison, as some girls arrived pregnant, their sentence often having been for hiding their boyfriends or husbands from the war. They were allowed to keep their babies with them for nine months, then they were given to German foster families. The partings were agony for the mothers, and while short monthly meetings were allowed afterwards, this only turned the knife as they saw their babies forget them and develop bonds with their new families.

It would be illness which would see Princesse Marie's release from Siegburg. Operations had been carried out there but many went wrong due to lack of proper cleanliness. When she first fell ill permission was initially refused for such treatment outside, but the Princesse knew the Germans were sticklers for rules and protocol and that she had the right to appeal. She did – to the Pope and the King of Spain, who intervened, and she was taken to Cologne for treatment and then for convalescence with nuns. One of her visitors was the city's Archbishop, who was perhaps returning a favour as the Princesse had treated his nephew's wounds after the Battle of Mons; another visitor was from a German branch of her family.

So these were the lives of David and Julie-Celestine during captivity in Germany: harsh and full of trouble. But in the outside world the war continued, and their fate along with that of millions of others would eventually be decided by its outcome. Rumour would have been just as rife within the prisons as everywhere else. Were worsening food rations evidence that Germany was struggling? Were the bad moods of their guards down to poor news from the front? All the captives could do was keep up their morale as best they could, try to survive and cling to the hope that all would turn out well.

Chapter 9

The War Ends

As 1918 dawned, David and Julie-Celestine were settling into their second year of captivity and, as they were receiving little accurate or reliable information, they had no possible way of knowing when it would end. There would perhaps have been the hope, or the prayer, that this year would see an Allied victory, but they had little on which to base such expectations. However, that year, which started like the previous one behind the walls and wire of the enemy, would prove to be climactic, bringing the conflict to a conclusion and seeing them liberated to return to what remained of their previous lives.

Germany's best chance of victory had always been speed, because of the problem otherwise of fighting on two fronts. The Schlieffen Plan had been the 'solution' to this problem, but it had failed and deadlock had ensued. Germany's allies had arguably been more of a hindrance than a help, needing frequent aid. 'It is like fighting shackled to a corpse,' was one German commander's blunt view of the Austrians. Whatever Germany tried had ended in failure: gas at Ypres in 1915, the assault on Verdun in 1916 and the attempt to deliver a knockout blow on the Eastern Front. The 'big idea' for 1917 had been to reintroduce submarine warfare to the Atlantic in order to starve Britain into submission, an 'unrestricted' campaign with anything afloat a target. It was a gamble because this could draw America into the conflict. So far the US had stayed neutral and President Woodrow Wilson had been re-elected in 1916 on a platform of keeping the country out of the war which would remain his policy for the time being. The sinking of the liner *Lusitania* in 1915 by a U-boat off the Irish coast, with 124 American citizens among the 1,000 passengers lost, had disgusted the Americans, and Germany had afterwards backpedalled on its U-boat campaign. But Germany was now desperate and some of her leaders were willing to do whatever was necessary to try and bring the war to a successful end.

It was very much a 'gambler's throw of the dice' by the Germans, and part of the gamble was that even if America did enter the war, Germany would have it won in Europe before the Americans could do much about it. In this thinking there was some logic, as the US Army was tiny in 1917, only about 200,000 men and with little combat experience, especially of anything like the battles which had been raging in Europe for the last three years. This American force also lacked necessary equipment and was many thousands of miles away, separated by a huge ocean from the major battlefields and initially, in any case, with few means of getting there. Consequently, the Germans were hatching a plan to bribe Mexico into war against the US. There was a recent history of conflict between the US and Mexico and relations were still tender. Mexico was promised bits of various American states as the reward for victory. The Germans made the offer in the 'Zimmerman Telegram' sent via transatlantic cable under the ocean. But the British had cracked the German ciphers, were delighted with what they read and could not wait to pass the news into American hands. Within a week of receiving the information in the telegram America was at war with Germany.

The U-boats had tremendous early success. Many hundreds of thousands of tons of shipping destined to aid the Allies were lost, and it did seem that the German strategy might pay off. Britain was allegedly within six weeks of starvation in the spring of 1917. Something had to be done, and that something was the third offensive at Ypres with the aim of finally breaking out of the Ypres Salient and pushing on all the way to the Belgian coast, from where it was believed many U-boats were operating. However, the Battle of Passchendaele between 31 July and early November failed to achieve a breakthrough and much of the fighting was done in appalling weather, transforming the already battered lowlands into a quagmire. The combined losses of both sides were half a million men. While the Germans may have felt some satisfaction that their Belgian coastline remained secure, in what had become a war of attrition they were now desperately short of manpower, especially on the Western Front.

However, as 1917 ended the outlook was not all bleak for Germany. In the east there had been real cause for jubilation and optimism. By the beginning of 1917 all most ordinary Russians wanted was an end to war, even if this meant seeing the back of the

Romanov dynasty. Matters came to a head that spring, when a revolution ousted the Tsar, resulting in the installation of a moderate government under Kerensky and his Mensheviks, but one pledged to fight on. It was not the end of Russia's troubles, though, and the Germans still hoped for a complete Russian collapse. For Kerensky's was a fragile government, and the opposition to it was strong and motivated, none more so than the Bolsheviks led by the revolutionary Lenin, whom the Germans had smuggled into Russia from his exile in Switzerland in the hope that he would foment discontent and possibly even more. Lenin understood exactly the mood of the mass of Russians and his promise of 'peace and bread' was now the only thing they heeded. A second revolution, led by the Bolsheviks, broke out in the autumn and displaced Kerensky. The Bolshevik government sued for peace and Russia's world war was over.

The new year of 1918 was now seen as critical by both sides. America was in, but it was going to be some time before she could bring sufficient numbers to Europe to cause the Germans any major difficulties. Closer to the action, both geographically and emotionally, were the German troops who had been fighting in the east against the Russians. These were plentiful, experienced and battle-hardened and now also buoyed by victory. Germany believed that her hour had arrived and that these men would be the instrument of total victory. It would not all be plain sailing, since the British and French were still in the fight and determined to continue. Moreover, a war-winning German offensive could not wait forever, because the Americans were beginning to sort out the necessary logistics. No major campaign could take place in the winter, but the US lines of supply and support were established regardless, and by the arrival of the New Year the fresh and keen drafts of Uncle Sam's men were arriving in Europe at the rate of 100,000 a month. The Germans had to act. They knew it, and so did the Allies.

David and Julie-Celestine, despite their incarceration, could not have been completely unaware of wider happenings in the war. Supplies, never lavish to start with, were becoming more meagre as the months passed, due to the British naval blockade. All Germans were feeling the strain of the war; whether it was lack of food and fuel, grieving for their war dead or worry about loved ones at the front, it was etched in their faces. As a generally disciplined people, they believed their leaders' promise that the sacrifices would ultimately be worthwhile and victory would come. They were told that their enemies were suffering more and barely hanging on. Certainly, anyone connected to POWs might have seen through this, since parcels from home to Germany contained goods the likes of which German civilians had not seen for a long time. But the Russian surrender was confirmation to many that victory was actually nearer now. Camp and prison guards would undoubtedly have crowed the news to their captives in the hope that it would further demoralize them.

The time was near. Germany knew she had to act quickly and use any temporary numerical advantage to its maximum potential. Over the winter of 1917/18 troops were moved from the now quiet eastern front to the west. Alongside their ordinary fighting men, experienced and battle hardened, the Germans were now going to try a tactic which had showed promise in the east. It was based on specially selected men, the fittest, keenest and bravest, who would be given special rations and chosen to spearhead any new attack. They were known as 'storm troops' and their mission would be to shock and awe the enemy and blast a path through on which their comrades would follow. Specially armed and trained for speed, they would bypass any hold-ups in order to cause as much chaos as possible in the enemy's rear areas of communication and supply. Their assault would be preceded by a bombardment the like of which the Allies had never experienced before. Its planner was Georg Bruchmüller, and so confident were the Germans that they allowed themselves a touch of Teutonic humour and nicknamed him 'Durchbruchmüller' – *Durchbruch* meaning 'breakthrough' in German.

The British and French knew that the Germans would plan and launch a major spring offensive, more than likely with newly-arrived reinforcements from the east. The question was, could they hold this massive onslaught? They feared it might be a close-run thing. Although conscription had been in force for many years now, there was concern that there might not be enough troops to meet the coming offensive. The only bit of the equation the Allies did not know was exactly where and when the assault would take place, although as it happened, the British could not have played into the Germans' hands any more if they had tried. Always of the greatest concern to the British were their lines of communication and supply back to the Channel ports, and it was these they were always likely to defend most stoutly. The French had a different preoccupation, however. For them Paris was paramount and they would do almost anything to protect their capital. There had been previous attempts by the Germans to drive a wedge between their foes and they knew the likely reaction of both.

The thinly-spread British were now holding some 130 miles of the Western Front. But along the British lines there had been rumblings of discontent in early 1918, chiefly from Sir Hubert Gough, whose Fifth Army was holding the longest stretch of line and also the one furthest from the coast. He was alarmed not only by his apparent shortage of men, but also by his lack of defensive materiel. To some degree the shortage of manpower was common to the whole British Army, due to the losses already sustained and the numbers needed at home by vital industries. But there was a political reason too. The Prime Minister, David Lloyd George, mistrusted the ability of his C-in-C Douglas Haig and believed his command would deliver little other than more names to the casualty lists. Lloyd George had a possible solution to this: keep Haig short of available men so that he could not get his hands on them and send them to their deaths in, from Lloyd George's point of view, pointless offensives. This may have been a good political strategy but it was about to have serious consequences on the battlefield.

Gough's pessimism and his fear that his section of the line would be chosen by the Germans was correct, but he was alone, for British High Command believed more tempting targets lay further north. Gough's front had indeed been quiet for a large part of the war, but this did not ease his fears. His call for more men and extra resources fell on deaf ears, but he did what he could in the circumstances and just had to hope for the best. One of his precautions was to build redoubt positions supporting each other but not actually physically linked. Almost like little islands of resistance, these were placed for best advantage and wired as strongly as possible. It was hoped that holding these fort-like positions lightly with men but with maximum firepower could break up and slow down any attack sufficiently to get reserves forward to deal with it. That may have been the plan, but these positions were unpopular with the men, who felt isolated, being more comfortable with the idea of fighting as a line. Also it unwittingly played into the Germans' hands: they hoped that the brutal artillery bombardment would nullify most enemy defences, but their main emphasis was placed on causing destruction and confusion in the rear, especially at command and control level. Surviving strong points like Gough's redoubts were simply to be bypassed by the storm troops, and others coming behind would deal with these isolated positions.

The Germans decided with some bombast to call this offensive the *Kaiserschlacht* (Kaiser's battle) and they put great faith in it. At best it might just win the war for them at a stroke, but even if it did not it might hammer their tired and demoralized enemies sufficiently to decide enough was enough and sue for peace on German terms. And it would all be achieved before the US had time to put its shoulder fully to the wheel. Then, with the Western Front no longer in existence, the Americans would find it hard to fight the Germans and therefore would undoubtedly settle too, so was the belief. Some German leaders, both military and civilian, felt uneasy, however, believing there was an element of desperation to this offensive, which far from ending the war might actually push the nation and people too far and finally over the edge to defeat. It was time to do or die.

The expected hammer blow duly fell in front of St Quentin on the morning of 21 March. The German achievement of surprise was almost total (except perhaps to Gough!), and the attackers were even helped by the weather as a thick fog covered the entire battlefield, hiding the assault and blinding any defence which survived the tremendous shelling. Given the amount of high explosive they threw at the British positions in the five-hour pre-dawn bombardment, accuracy was hardly an issue. The German gunners did not need visibility at all as they already knew their intended targets from map references and had their guns ranged and sighted perfectly. The fog in reality was a godsend to the Germans and further proof to them that this was going to be their day. Once again, the British cursed their bad luck as ever when it came to the weather. On both sides, however, there was no doubting that this was the real thing.

But following the military adage that no plan survives first contact with the enemy, it did not all go exactly as intended. The barrage was hell, causing many losses even before the infantry assault, but the

British remained their usual stubborn selves, relishing a seemingly overwhelming challenge, and as the Germans came on they met stiff resistance. The defenders believed their redoubts were 'hold at all cost' positions and surrender was not an option. Even when the Germans offered terms to surrounded positions and all hope was gone, the response was often a hail of bullets or grenades rather than a white flag. Despite previous evidence of British steadfastness, this defiance amazed and angered the Germans – and perhaps excited some admiration too. Due to the Germans' superiority in numbers they were always going to get through, but as in 1914 speed was vital, and if the attackers did not make rapid progress, it was going to be bad news for their strategy. The British instinctively knew this, and in their hearts so too did many Germans, but there was little for either side to do at the moment other than fight it out to the best of their abilities.

Gough now faced the greatest challenge of his military career: to hold and slow down the Germans, while at the same time keeping his force from being annihilated and then withdrawing in some order to fight another day when reinforced. It was Le Cateau all over again. His options were limited because he was always going to have to give ground when facing such a massive ongoing attack. There was no choice in this, but where to hold and when to move were the tricky points, as getting it wrong could mean disaster. Lloyd George's plan of keeping any available troops in Britain was now seen to be extremely flawed, and the process of sending out as many reinforcements as possible began immediately – including 50,000 eighteen-year-olds who officially were too young to be sent overseas (nineteen was the age at which a soldier could legally die for his country). Anyone who could hold a rifle was needed.

The Germans were so delighted with their opening day that the Kaiser himself moved closer to the front to congratulate everyone, exhort his troops to continue the effort and enjoy the long-awaited breakthrough as the hated British were finally and seemingly decisively defeated. For the British had been the main target of this battle. While 1916 had been about knocking France out of the war at Verdun, this battle was about beating Britain. The German belief was that French losses and low morale after so much exhausting struggle would see the nation crumble if the prop of British support was now knocked away. If a sufficient wedge could be driven between the two allies, the job would almost do itself, the Germans felt. They knew the British would fall back on the Channel ports and the French on Paris.

All parties realized that this could be the war's deciding point. The British appealed for French support and although it was sent, it came neither in the numbers nor at the speed which they felt necessary. The Germans had banked on disagreements among their strained adversaries, and all seemed to be going their way. In this crisis it was accepted finally that there must be a unified overall Allied command on the battlefields. What was needed now was a man of decision, vision and action. He would have to be French, all agreed, as France was where the main battleground was. But could such a man be found? Yes, he could, in the shape of Ferdinand Foch, who never doubted that however bleak the situation there would be final victory. He was just what was needed at this critical hour, as March ended and with it arguably Germany's last best chance. Critically, Germany had taken huge casualties and thus lost her numerical advantage.

As ever, it was a combination of factors that saw the Allies survive and the Germans halted. Staunch British defending certainly played its part, as well as resolute leadership. Reserves had been released just in time and helped steady the ship. But the condition of the German troops played a part too. Reference has already been made to the British naval blockade. Germany was running on empty, with the best of what little there was going to the armed forces. The troops had been fed the lie that the enemy was suffering even more. This was initially believed, but during the offensive German troops captured massive stores of Allied supplies, and the falsehood was cruelly exposed. Soldiers stopped to gorge themselves and drink excessively, and on many occasions their officers could not get them moving again speedily or usefully.

When the *Kaiserschlacht* failed, the effect was not only felt on the battlefield. While civilians back home, including no doubt the captors of David and Julie-Celestine, revelled in the early victories and recounted them to their prisoners, there was no hiding the fact that Germany had failed to deliver the knockout blow. The war would now grind on for who knew how long. And there was a devastating side effect: those German soldiers who had stopped to enjoy captured supplies had written home about them, not only to say that they had enjoyed the spoils, but also to complain that their leaders were lying; in reality, the enemy was lavishly provided for, not struggling. And if their leaders had lied about this, just what else they had said about the war might be untrue? Civilian morale started to collapse rapidly in the summer of 1918 as the *pfennig* finally dropped about the true plight of Germany. Strikes increased in the factories and political unrest focused on demands that the war be ended. This cannot have gone unheeded by the more observant inmates of camps and must have given their morale a tremendous boost.

Increasingly desperate lunges were made by the Germans at various points of the front later in the spring and into the early summer, all following a similar pattern: starting well but soon running out of steam and achieving little lasting advantage. The first of these came at Ypres in April; next came an assault in May on the old Chemin des Dames battlefield; then a summer offensive on the Marne which, while briefly threatening Paris, again failed like all the others. Losses were tremendous on both sides, but the Germans could no longer sustain them. By the summer Germany had effectively shot her bolt.

There was a huge collective sigh of relief from the Allies, who knew at times just how close it had been. In this stage of the war the Americans had started to feature and prove their worth; they were now arriving in Europe in ever increasing numbers. While some generals and politicians viewed this averted crisis as a chance to build up Allied forces for the final onslaught to take place in 1919 or perhaps 1920, Haig, and fortunately Foch too, saw things differently. They argued that if the Allies acted boldly then the war might be won in 1918. Their view prevailed, and on 8 August the last 100-day offensive was launched. It was decisive. While the Germans continued to defend their positions, they were not the same armies as before, and at home things were certainly spiralling downwards. As the defences of the mighty Hindenburg Line fell in September even the most optimistic German realized the end was nigh. Secret negotiations began, leading to the Kaiser's abdication and defection to neutral Holland and the signing of an Armistice, which came into force at 1100 hrs on 11 November at Compiègne.

Chapter 10

Going Home

Although the war was officially over, this was a moot point to many. In Germany, while defeat was a bitter pill there was also an almost collective national sigh of relief that the killing was through. Indeed, the state which had gone to war in 1914 no longer existed, with Kaiser Wilhelm having abdicated. The military leaders were discredited, but had slyly handed power back to a civilian government before the whole edifice collapsed – something which would have a devastating effect in later years when Hitler and his Nazis used the 'stab in the back' lie, that the new government had robbed Germany of its rightful victory. Not many saw it that way at the end of 1918. The military were certainly still active behind the scenes and would be vital if some semblance of law and order was to be preserved and the country prevented from undergoing a communist revolution as in Russia. Germany was now nominally a republic but anarchy ruled in many parts of the country, with workers and soldiers forming soviets or militant councils.

What the end of the war and all this chaos meant for prisoners of war varied from area to area. A veteran known to one of the authors said that POWs had generally been in the dark about how close the end was but knew something was afoot when their usually surly and dismissive commandant addressed them as 'gentlemen' for the first time. The next day, all the guards had melted away and the gates of the camp were left wide open. Sometimes officers announced that the war was over and as far as they were concerned prisoners were now free to leave. For guards who had ruled through terror there was perhaps a fear of retribution and so they quickly made themselves scarce, but the overriding sentiment among most guards was a desire to turn their back on the conflict, return to their loved ones and see what they could salvage from their pre-war lives. It was clearly going to be hard just to survive in this new and unknown Germany.

Under the terms of the newly signed Armistice former prisoners were now indeed free, but not many in Germany seemed too concerned with their plight. The Germans had enough problems of their own. But what this meant in real terms was more problematic. That all POWs wanted to get the hell out of there and back home was obvious, but it was sometimes easier said than done. The long and harsh period of privation had left some men too weak to consider moving quickly. Even though Red Cross parcels and packages from home had been their right, transportation problems and pilfering by desperate Germans meant parcels did not always arrive quickly or at all at their intended destinations. As well as hunger there was sickness, and the run-down condition of many men left them open to disease. The oncoming winter of 1918/19 was going to see the influenza pandemic which killed so many. It seemed cruel to have survived the war but then be robbed of the chance of repatriation by illness, but sadly it was a common fate.

Some men were lucky enough to be in camps close to the borders of other countries, and this meant that some former POWs simply left their camps and literally walked out of Germany. Others, bolder or more determined, took public transport if it was available or hitched rides. Cologne was a popular destination in the south-west as it was a major transport hub. Further north, they might head for Holland or make for the coast to try and take ship away from Germany. Generally there seems to have been little resentment or animosity against these foreigners out in the countryside or in smaller towns, but at least one group of ex-prisoners found themselves chased by a knife-wielding gang after reaching Cologne and had to take refuge offered by a sympathetic hotelier; other similar incidents were recorded elsewhere.

Some camp officers requested that their former charges stay where they were until proper provision could be made to get them away. Inmates who were ill, weak or simply too far away from borders, often accepted this as the best of a bad job. In reality, the Germans were perhaps not being as benign as they seemed. The Armistice was not the formal end of the war, only the opening of a period of negotiation which, theoretically at least, could have broken down and led to the recommencement of hostilities. This was not in reality likely to happen, given conditions in Germany and the mood of its army and population in general, but while the Germans still held prisoners they continued to have some bargaining power. On the other side of the coin, no German prisoners were allowed to go free under the terms of the Armistice. So the Germans were also effectively playing tit-for-tat, and one of the excuses they made was that the Allied demand for trains and rolling stock to be turned over to them made returning prisoners difficult. There were eighty-eight ambulance trains on the books but only eight were fit for use, it was said. Medical supervision was also sketchy, and one train arriving in Cologne was found to have 33 dead men among 512 former POWs.

The slowness of repatriation is reflected in figures showing that fewer than ten per cent of former British POWs had made it back to their own shores by the end of November. By the middle of December half were now at least in Allied camps, but even at the start of the New Year estimates put 14,000 former troops still in German hands. It should be borne in mind that these are only the statistics for British soldiers and do not include the other nationalities who had been fighting the Germans. Progress was far too slow for many, and so Red Cross units were sent into Germany to find, assess and make arrangements for men still held in the twenty-one Army districts of the country; but even then it was not until early February that everyone was away. The main ports used in France were Calais and Boulogne, but neutral ports such as Rotterdam in Holland and Copenhagen in Denmark were also used. Great as it must have been for the rescued men to leave, and even better to see Dover, Hull or Leith coming into view, it was not yet the end of the saga. Before going home there were dispersal camps, formalities to be undergone and interviews about their treatment in Germany with a view to possible war crimes charges against their former captors. The process must have seemed interminable to men who just wanted to get back to their loved ones.

In all of this, David was luckier than most; he seems to have had a relatively problem-free release and return home and he was back in Glasgow within a month of the Armistice having been signed – 2 December to be exact. Whether he made it back through official channels or under his own steam is unknown, but given that he ended up so quickly in Glasgow, rather than perhaps heading back to Le Cateau, it was probably an officially sanctioned journey. Once home, there would undoubtedly have been a wonderful family reunion, but he was still in the Army so there were details which needed to be hammered out and perhaps one or two questions answered.

A fellow inmate of David's at Soltau for part of 1918 was former Royal Inniskilling Fusilier, Drummer Samuel Kydd from Londonderry. He lost his unit on 24 August 1914 when a bolting mule pulled him between the lines, and he hid in a drain. He did fall in with about 400 other British soldiers of various units, but there was little leadership from officers. They were ordered first to Le Cateau, then to St Quentin, then told to fend for themselves. Kydd decided to make for Ham but, confused and exhausted (he later said, 'We were completely stupid, not knowing what to do'), they then came under shellfire which killed and wounded some of them. At one point he feigned death as Germans ran by him. After they passed he went and hid in a wood with other soldiers, both British and French. An old man brought them some food and civilian clothes, and he thought he might be able to get back to the British lines.

He quickly found that this was easier said than done. Hunger forced him into a restaurant where a local woman guessed he was British; she beckoned him to follow her to a house where he stayed unhappily for six days, because he was locked in during the day and saw the woman 'fooling around with German soldiers' outside. Then another woman came with an English-French dictionary, told him it was unsafe there and took him to another house, where she lived with her sister. Her name was Mme Veut Lorette and he stayed with her for two and a half years. A local priest was in on the secret and managed to get letters passed between him and other soldiers hiding locally. He was to break the bad news that two of them, Thomas Hands and John Hughes, had been discovered and shot by the Germans in early March 1915.

The tightening German vice and ever more threatening proclamations meant Kydd finally decided to give himself up. The sisters had got him false papers and suggested he try to pass himself off as French, but he soon realized it was hopeless. After German questioning, at which he was vague and evasive, he was badly beaten. The Germans had the sisters' address, but he told them nothing. The next day he was taken to their street in handcuffs. One of the sisters was in the front garden. A German put a pistol to Kydd's head and asked her if she had hidden this man; she replied that she had. A trial followed and Kydd got ten years in prison. He said that life at Soltau was very tough, with long working days.

Kydd's route home was circuitous and not without incident. Revolutionary guards took over the camp and the inmates were marched to another, where he caught the flu which was raging then and killed hundreds of those awaiting release. He survived and at Christmas was sent to Hameln, from where daily drafts were being dispatched to Holland. A sense of Kydd's delight comes from his description of his departure. He borrowed a cornet from another former POW and blew the Last Post when crossing the border. 'We were mad with leaving the old Hunland,' he said, and three days later he was back in Blighty.

An insight into the ending of Julie-Celestine's nightmare may be gained from the experiences of the Princesse Marie de Croy, her fellow detainee at Siegburg prison. She wrote:

> After a few days of breathless suspense, we heard that the Armistice had been signed, and almost simultaneously the prisoners were to be returned to their respective countries. Frau Manser arrived suddenly to tell me that, the day before, a delegation of soldiers, sailors and workers had summoned the Direction to throw the doors open, threatening them with death if they refused. These revolutionaries had taken the keys and opened all the cells . . . Our women, who had known very little about outside events, were so taken by surprise at the idea of being free that they had not dared to stay and claim their property . . . but had rushed out as they were.

The Princesse said that she saw little violence but that one former warder was thrown out of a window and broke her neck.

Julie-Celestine's route and the timing of her return have not been recorded, but she had proved already many times that she was a determined and resourceful woman and she would doubtless have wanted to get back as quickly as possible. Princesse Marie did record her journey, however, and she encountered many fellow returnees making the same one. Incredibly, or perhaps not, since Germany remained efficient even in defeat, the trains were still running, albeit sporadically, and many freed prisoners tried to get to Cologne, which was a major rail centre and also close to the border. The station became a magnet for those wishing to get away, but it was not without its dangers, as there were revolutionaries everywhere, as well as soldiers, all armed and many of them drunk. The Princesse, who made it to Cologne by evening, found the station packed with them, revelling and asking everyone to dance. Also there she saw the other side of the coin of the now politically divided Germany: banners across the streets which read 'Welcome to our unconquered armies'. No train was available across the border until the next day so she found a hotel she had stayed in before the war and where, incredibly, the staff remembered her. A meal was available but consisted of only two small potatoes and meat she suspected was dog.

In the morning she caught a train heading for Spa in Belgium, but the journey was not without incidents, the chief of which was being shot at from another locomotive pulling carriages full of 'Reds' (communists), one of many full of troops she saw steaming back into Germany. Just before the border she had to change trains and she joined a new one full of ragged returning French and Belgian soldiers who, she said, were in the best of spirits as might be expected. Eventually she arrived in Louvain, where crowds were cheering the exit of the Germans, and she saw her first 'free' Belgian soldier; she was so overjoyed that she ran over to shake hands with him. At Louvain she also met four British ex-prisoners who looked like beggars in their odd collections of bits of uniform and civilian clothing and assorted footwear ranging from clogs to slippers. They told her that they were POWs who had been forced to work several months for the German army, until set loose that morning and told that they were free. As well as being ragged, they looked like they had not seen a good meal for a long time, and the Princesse made herself very popular when she got a shopkeeper to offer them tea, pastries and biscuits. On hearing that she had been involved with Nurse Cavell, they all solemnly stood up and insisted on shaking her hand.

The Princesse then travelled to Brussels and stayed at nearby Jolimont with noble friends who were delighted to have just been reunited with their son, whom they had not seen since war had been declared. Double joy came when another son returned who had also been imprisoned at Siegburg. The Princesse sought news of her own home, but there was none. Her friends took her to Brussels to witness the royal family returning to the capital, and soon afterwards she was presented, in borrowed clothes, to the Queen, who wanted to hear her story and listened, the Princesse said, with rapt attention as she described what she had been through and how other Belgian prisoners had bravely endured their hardships. But probably the happiest moments of her early freedom came when she caught up accidentally with her brother Leopold, who had not known his sister was in the capital; in fact, he had no idea where she was at all, but a mutual friend gave him the happy news and there was a joyful reunion. Another happy meeting came via the Queen herself, who fixed it for another brother, Reginald, to be allowed some leave from his duties in London to see his sister for the first time in four years.

The following month, a visit was arranged to her former home. Progress was slow over the bad roads, but eventually they reached the chateau to find it holed in places and with craters in the lawns but deemed sufficiently habitable to serve as the billet for officers of the 15th Bedfordshire Regiment, who promptly invited her to stay for dinner! She had not seen the house since 1914 and said she felt like Alice in Wonderland, never more so than when sat in her own home, surrounded by these friendly strangers and with a massive unexploded shell awaiting removal by the Royal Engineers in the middle of the room. She had hoped to stay but swiftly realized this was impossible so returned to Brussels until sufficient repairs could be made.

Without royal connections or previous acquaintance with German hotel staff, with little command of the German language other than what she may have picked up in prison, and undoubtedly with little in the way of money following her release, Julie-Celestine's return would certainly have differed from that of the Princesse; but she did make it back to Le Cateau to discover what had happened to her family and home during her absence. The war had been won but there was now going to be many a battle ahead just to try and survive the victory, never mind getting back to any kind of normal life, if indeed that would ever be possible.

Chapter 11

Reunions

The town to which Julie-Celestine returned after her two-year absence was very different to the one she had been forcibly taken away from as a prisoner and must often have wondered if she would ever see again. There had been a second battle of Le Cateau in early October 1918 as the Germans were harried on their way to surrender during the final 'Hundred Days' of the war, and the town had suffered its share of shelling on this occasion. The damage had been nothing compared to that inflicted on towns such as Ypres in Belgium or Albert on the Somme, but sadly the pre-war Baudhuin family home had been a victim. While the town was delighted to be finally done with the occupation and reunited with the rest of France, it was going to be some considerable time before anything would be 'normal' again – if that was indeed ever going to be possible. As well as the physical damage to homes, workplaces and the infrastructure generally, the people were malnourished and tired, and a hard winter beckoned.

Bricks and mortar could eventually be replaced, but some of the losses due to the war were irrevocable. There were emotional reunions in the new home found in Le Cateau for Julie-Celestine and her husband Jules, who was one of those ragged French POWs making his way back at the time. Perhaps the couple even took the same route. Their son Léon also came back from his sentence of forced labour imposed by the Germans, hopefully a rather easier journey since he had not left France. Both Jules and Léon were in a poor physical state due to their privations, but worst of all was the condition of the youngest member of the family, Marie, who had been left alone following her mother's arrest and imprisonment. Sympathetic locals had rallied round and done their best for her, but food was scarce, she had been left completely traumatized by her experiences and in truth she would never completely recover. But these were perhaps the lucky ones. The Baudhuins' oldest child, Jules junior, would never be returning home because he had been killed in action – a fate shared by some 1.4 million Frenchmen. In time, the family was officially informed that his remains had been buried and marked by tomb number 558 in the Courbesseaux Cemetery at Harcourt in the Meurthe et Moselle département, some 200 miles from his home.

France had been ravaged by the Great War in a way that no one who did not witness it could ever imagine. And the destruction had been savagely concentrated mostly in just one part of the country, the north-east. While the cost in soldiers' lives had been shared throughout the nation, the areas which had been fought over paid the heaviest price in terms of property and environment. In the areas where there had been stalemate for almost the entire war, and where literally millions of shells had been fired by both sides, it is no exaggeration to say that it was hard to tell that humanity had ever existed there. After the fighting the authorities classified areas in terms of damage suffered, and the worst were declared *zones rouges* – red zones, where it was expected that no one would live again. The ground devastated in the fighting around Verdun was classified as such, and the whole area was planted as forestry, with the nine villages blown off the face of the earth never rebuilt.

A document called *le bilan de la guerre* – the bill of war – was produced, which in cold hard figures detailed exactly what it promised: the cost of this war for France. In truth, there were many costs. In money terms the total bill was 1,126,594 million francs. Cultivated land amounting to 1.7 million hectares had been devastated, as well as a further 2 million of non-cultivated. The number of communes registering complete destruction stood at 1,699, a figure almost equalled by those with 50 per cent damage; a further 707 put their ruin at 75 per cent. There had been 20,603 factories lost, 52,754km of road, 8,000km of railways, 4,875 bridges and 12 tunnels. As grim as this bill was, however, all these things could in time and with effort be replaced.

While victory had been achieved, it still came back to the question of the human cost, especially in terms of those who were no longer around to enjoy it. And while this toll had fallen heaviest on the military, there had been a huge civilian cost too: people killed by shelling, in enemy atrocities, by illness as a result of poor supply of food and medicines – as well as those taken away by the Germans into prison or to work and who had subsequently died. One inhabitant in every twenty-seven in France was killed during the war – as compared to one in fifty-two in Britain and one in thirty in Germany. The *bilan* broke it all down: four French soldiers died for every minute of the war, 240 per hour and 6,400 for each and every day. If the war dead were to form fours and march as battalions past a fixed point every seven and half minutes, it would take eighty-one days and nights for them all to pass. If their coffins were piled on top of the Arc de Triomphe they would form a column reaching 110 times the height of the memorial up to 5.5km in the sky – 700m taller than France's highest mountain, Mont Blanc.

Le Cateau might not have suffered the sheer physical damage of some other French towns, but it had been knocked about by the war. Much of its previous workforce had been killed or disabled and it was going to take the civil authorities some time to get to grips with all the problems ahead. There would need to be considerable government support for such communities before any semblance of normal life could be lived again. Temporary wooden hut-type houses, soon dubbed 'barracks', were thrown up for the homeless. In some parts of the battlefields people lived in the bunkers and dugouts left behind by the troops. The winter of 1918/19 was looming as the Armistice was signed on 11 November. The national French franc did not make an immediate return and locally produced currencies quickly replaced the hated money imposed by the Germans in the formerly occupied area. But the one thing these French northerners were renowned for throughout the country was their stoicism and ability to knuckle down and work hard. The former quality had been much in evidence during the war and occupation. Now both were going to be put to the test again.

Far from Le Cateau, as the dust settled and the true enormity of what lay ahead became clear, there was a former resident champing at the bit to get back. He had not been born or bred there; indeed, his stay of just two years had been neither a voluntary nor a totally pleasant one. But in Glasgow David Cruickshank was pulling out all the stops to try and make a return there as quickly as possible. This was easier said than done, for he was still officially a soldier in the British Army and so had no free choice in such matters. In truth, it was not actually Le Cateau itself or its people in general that David was missing, but a certain one of its inhabitants. During his incarceration he had never forgotten his beautiful girlfriend Aimée Olivier; nor had she forgotten him, and they simply could not wait to see each other again. Even though technically the war had not legally ended – and would not do so until the signing of the Treaty of Versailles in June 1919 – it was going to take more than a mere world war to keep the young lovers apart for much longer.

And so it proved. Even though still apart, the couple could now communicate freely and they were desperately keen to make up for lost time and get together again as quickly as possible. Their love could so easily not have survived after all they had endured, but it did and despite everything it had flourished. Aimée was a beautiful girl and certainly would not have been without suitors while David was away. Many other girls in similar circumstances would have faltered. But she remained steadfast and true, and when David suggested that as their love had survived so much it was evident that they were meant to be together forever, she immediately agreed to his proposal of marriage, tricky as the realization of it may have seemed.

But as the saying goes, love will find a way – and this proved to be the case. Even though David was a serving soldier and not long back from the Continent, the military authorities gave him dispensation to return to France and marry his sweetheart. Perhaps he already knew this would be the case when he made his proposal. And so, just a day over three months after the Armistice was signed, on 12 February 1919, David and Aimée with a few of her family and well-wishers gathered in the town hall of the war-scarred Le Cateau for their wedding. French weddings mostly take this form, rather than a church service, as it is the civil ceremony which is the binding one.

Their wedding certificate has survived in the local archives and makes interesting reading. Officiating was the town's Deputy Mayor, M Emile Picard, who during the occupation had carried out so many important acts of resistance in the service of his town and its residents while the Mayor himself had been imprisoned as a hostage by the Germans. He is listed as being a *Chevalier de la Legion d'Honneur*, one of his nation's highest awards. The beautifully handwritten document gives David's full name, including his middle moniker

Waddell, lists his occupation as a soldier of the Cameronians S.R. (Scottish Rifles) and comes complete with his place and date of birth. However, not for the first time and probably not the last, he is recorded as English, since the author of the document was of the opinion that Glasgow was in England. David's parents and their occupations and home address are also listed. Aimée's details are then made out in the same way, giving her occupation as weaver and her place of residence as Le Cateau. As Aimée's father Théodore was dead, permission for the marriage was given by her aunt Angéline Place, a carer from Le Cateau.

There was no one from David's Scottish family at the wedding, perhaps not surprisingly given its location and timing, but Aimée had several relatives present, many of whom signed the document after the happy couple. Another witness, fittingly, was Léon Basquin, who had also risked so much on behalf of British escapees. Finally, making it all legal, comes the signature of Emile Picard, and so the no doubt happy couple were married at last. It must have seemed almost unbelievable after all they had gone through.

Given the absence of David's family on the big day, the happy couple then took the opportunity to go back to Glasgow so his family could meet their new daughter-in-law for the first time. A photograph from this visit has survived which shows them with David's mother. The groom is in his army uniform with his Glengarry and Cameronians badge. Close scrutiny of David's uniform reveals a few interesting details. Above the cuff of his left sleeve can be seen two good conduct stripes, which show that he had had an unblemished career as far as the army was concerned and that he had five years service under his belt to the month (he had joined up in February 1914). Just visible on his other sleeve are the overseas service chevrons, which had been brought in by the military in December 1917. There was one for every year abroad and David appears to have the full set. It seems the Army was happy to consider his time disguised as Mademoiselle Louise and behind German prison or camp bars as no hindrance to qualification. Over his left tunic pocket is the ribbon for the 1914 Star medal, which had also been approved in 1917. Also known unofficially as the Mons Star, it was only issued to soldiers who had served in France or Belgium from 5 August up to midnight on 22 November 1914.

But while this new family celebrated, another one central to this story was conspicuous by its absence. David had of course become very much part of this other family, the Baudhuins, while he had been hidden for so long in Le Cateau – a family that had risked its very existence by caring for and protecting him, going without and knowing the price of discovery. Its matriarch, Julie-Celestine, had actually risked her own life for a second time when she stood up in a German military tribunal to plead for the life of the young man she declared emotionally she had come to regard as her own son. The Baudhuins had brought Aimée into David's life, too, and supported the blossoming love affair. But neither Julie-Celestine nor any other member of the Baudhuin clan felt they could go along to the town hall to see David and Aimée wed.

The Baudhuin matriarch had clearly had a major change of heart since that day in court in the autumn of 1916. What had triggered such a reaction? Had her time in harsh German captivity caused her to change her view of David? It is not known if there was any exchange of letters between the two during their respective incarcerations. If not, this could have been the problem, with Julie-Celestine believing she had risked and lost so much for nothing. Had she been cut to the quick by the lack of news from David as the war ended? David's love for Aimée had surely not gone unheeded in the family, and it should have come as no surprise that the lovers wanted to be reunited as soon as possible. But did David actually inform her of his intentions to marry Aimée or did she hear this from another source first? From David's point of view at least, the first person he had to get in touch with on his liberation, and then see on his return to Le Cateau, would have been his fiancée. Did all this put Julie-Celestine's nose out of joint so that she reacted in this most dramatic way?

The truth is, sadly, that we do not know. No firm evidence has yet come to light about the reason for the dispute. We can make all the suppositions we like, but the two major protagonists never spoke publically about it and the question was never posed to them in any of the interviews they gave – or if put, it went unanswered. In the less intrusive era of the 1920s and 1930s interviewers were less likely to delve into the private lives of their subjects. But the pain must have gone deep – especially for Julie-Celestine. It is hard to imagine why

David could possibly have fallen out with her after all she had done for him. Whether any bridge-building was attempted by the young Scotsman again remains unknown, but hurt can often be a two-way process and when combined with other emotions such as pride, perhaps even jealousy, can make a combustible mixture. Le Cateau authority and writer Jean-Marc Caudron, in the December 1996 edition of the local history magazine *Jadis en Cambresis*, certainly speculated that it was the possessive character of Julie-Celestine which was at the root of the problem. The single documented fact that does emerge about this sad turn of events comes from the marriage certificate, which states that no one had registered any opposition to it taking place – so the new Mr and Mrs Cruickshank were about to start their married life together. But the falling out must have been painful for everyone concerned, and in such a small community their paths were always likely to cross and keep the hurt alive.

One person David was not going to have any more problems with, or cross paths with again in Le Cateau, was the infamous Madame D who had betrayed him to the enemy. It must have been with a certain element of satisfaction that he found himself called as a prosecution witness at her trial. In March 1919 the local journal carried an article with the headline, 'A Friend of the Krauts in Cambrai, Douai and Lens', which told of the arrest in Paris of a Jeanne Dave. The charges were that she had often travelled to Lille, the regional capital and major German HQ, had reported events in the headlined towns as well as betraying a soldier (presumably David) and had 'entertained relations with numerous German officers'. That she had been arrested in Paris suggests she had perhaps tried to lose herself in the big city, as her activities and whereabouts would soon have become widely known in little Le Cateau. David said that all the evidence at the trial had been conclusive and Madame D was sentenced to death.

David would remain officially a soldier in the British Army until 9 December 1919. This can be said with certainty as it is the date on his official Medal Index Card, which has survived and lists the awards to which he was entitled due to his service. As well as the so-called Mons Star, whose ribbon he wore on his tunic in his wedding photo, he was also due and issued with the British War Medal and the Victory Medal. It was a full set as far as soldiers of the Great War were concerned, other than gallantry or bravery awards, since no campaign medals or bars were given for individual battles. While soldiers were mostly proud enough to have them, the disparaging humour of the Tommies was still to the fore and the trio soon become affectionately known as Pip, Squeak and Wilfred after a popular newspaper cartoon strip featuring the adventures of a dog, a penguin and a rabbit. Also noted is the entitlement to the clasp of roses which would be worn with the ribbon bar to the 1914 Star.

As well as this information, the Medal Index Card also gives the reason for David's discharge from the army, not in actual words but as a King's Regulations abbreviation which when translated means 'discharged as no longer physically fit for war service'. So that was that, then. Even if David had perhaps been thinking of staying on in the army and signing up for another term – he was a Regular after all – the decision had been made for him. There would be the tying up of loose ends such as payments and other formalities, but he was now a free man. And as a newly liberated and married man this probably suited him just fine.

The start of their married life for the young couple could not have been much more difficult. But they had survived and endured when so many others they had known had not, and they were young and resilient with, most importantly now, a future together stretching out ahead. They could finally express their love fully, openly and without fear. Life was certainly not going to be easy wherever they chose to settle, whether it meant returning to Scotland or remaining in still war-shattered northern France, but they had faith in the future and in each other. In their eyes there was much to look forward to – and together they were sure that they could achieve anything.

Chapter 12

Back to Work

With decent paid work hard to find for native Frenchmen as the war ended, one would have thought it virtually impossible for a foreigner, even if David did not consider himself such after his long, albeit enforced, stay in the country. Moreover, he had been a soldier fighting for France's liberation, even if his front line service had only lasted a few days. He had shared the people's dangers and hardships during the occupation and, after his betrayal and discovery, if the tribunal's initial sentence had been carried out, he would have died for France; and to underline his credentials as an adopted Frenchman, he had returned at the earliest possible opportunity and married his local sweetheart. He would have had some Army pay and entitlements, so his need might not have been as pressing as that of many, but he was going to need some kind of proper paid work before too long.

Luckily for David, the Imperial War Graves Commission was recruiting, and as a young, locally-based former soldier he had just the kind of CV it was looking for. The Commission had its roots in the years of war thanks to the far-sightedness of an early Red Cross volunteer called Fabian Ware. At forty-five, Ware was too old to enlist and fight but, a driven character who had travelled widely and worked in business, education and journalism, he decided he had to do something for the war effort and was soon overseas with a unit tending the wounded. Sadly, of course, the wounded did not always recover, and Ware was moved by the graves of the fallen. He enquired what records were being kept of these, and the answer was none. The Army had a responsibility for burials, but while individual units might keep records, it was all a bit haphazard. Ware thought this a terrible omission. Relatives of the fallen at home should at least have the consolation that their loved ones were in known graves which were being cared for. It was not just a question of respect for their sacrifice but of morale for everyone concerned. Soldiers, too, were already tending the graves of their mates. Perhaps in time photographs could be sent to grieving families showing that graves and cemeteries were being cared for. And if these were centrally registered they could be found after the war, even if records were lost in subsequent actions. Undoubtedly there would also be many people wanting to visit these sacred sites.

Then there were the cases of men missing. Right from the war's beginning many fell into this category, and for their families at home this was perhaps even worse than the certainty of a battlefield death. Official channels of information existed but were slow. Ware saw this problem very clearly and immediately took on the role of trying to make improvements to the system. Sadly, recording the dead efficiently often quashed the hope that a missing soldier might turn up, but at least families were no longer left in limbo. Ware's mobile unit ranged far and wide under the internationally recognized protection of the Red Cross, and he firmly told the military authorities that while he would co-operate with the Army fully he would remain independent of it. Such was his drive that he quickly secured more vehicles and resources from home for his work. Graves were now being actively sought and registered and a regime of maintenance set up.

Higher authorities and officialdom soon noticed his skill and efficiency. The Army was being besieged with letters from desperate families hoping for news, and so the Adjutant General of the BEF, General Sir Nevil Macready, readily agreed to a meeting requested by Ware. He had long been a soldier and remembered the huge public distress when the neglected state of Boer War graves had been discovered. He and Ware were clearly on the same wavelength, and when the civilian suggested that as his organization was already carrying out this important work it should be given the formal recognition and resources to go with it, Macready readily agreed and wrote to the C-in-C, Sir John French, to obtain permission from the War Office for approval of a graves registration unit to be incorporated into the Army. This was granted on 2 March 1915, when Ware's organization officially became the Graves Registration Commission.

Another early convert and supporter was Corps Commander Sir Douglas Haig, who would later that year replace Sir John as the BEF chief. Although not noted in some quarters as a sympathetic soul, Sir Douglas wrote to the War Office:

It is fully recognized that the work of the organization is of purely sentimental value, and that it does not directly contribute to the successful termination of the war. It has, however, an extraordinary moral value to the troops as well as to the relatives and friends of the dead at home . . . Further, on the termination of hostilities, the nation will demand an account from the government as to the steps which have been taken to mark and classify the burial places for the dead.

After the war, Haig would also clearly consider the living as well since he came to head the newly formed British Legion seeking better care for veterans.

Ware was made a temporary officer with the rank of major in the new unit which, while still with the Red Cross, was now also part of the Adjutant General's office in the Army. He set about his new role with gusto and recorded some 27,000 graves that year alone. But it soon became clear to him that it would aid the efficiency of the organization tremendously if it were to sever its link with the Red Cross and be completely taken over by the Army; the ever-obliging General Macready duly got the required War Office permission for just that in September.

As the initially mobile war settled into stalemate, burials had inevitably become less scattered and more concentrated. The first burials had often taken place in local churchyards and civilian cemeteries, but these were filling up and Ware realized another solution was needed. As a fluent French speaker he was just the man to take up the matter with the authorities, and his persuasive powers soon brought about an agreement for the creation of special communal plots to be given to both French and other Allied dead. This programme started in 1916, when locations were chosen and one of the Commission's most basic principles was instituted, that the sites would be cared for 'in perpetuity'. Other principles, that there would be equality of commemoration with no exception to rank and no repatriation of bodies, were also quickly advocated by Ware and accepted on the battlefield – if not by some of the public after the war who understandably wanted their loved ones home. This delicate issue was only officially settled in 1920. One of the fallen did return that year with his nation's backing– the Unknown Warrior, to be buried at Westminster Abbey.

Immediately on the creation of cemeteries, often in lands still ravaged by war, great efforts were made to present them as places of respect and remembrance. Grass was sown where possible and flowers planted. Photographs were taken on request. Ware's view was that these men had died for their country and the very least their country could do for them and their families now was to look after their graves. While the war raged this was the only option, but he hoped that afterwards the work should be maintained officially and not farmed out to a commercial body which might put profit and return before anything worthier and more lasting.

Luckily, Ware had an enthusiastic and powerful ally who shared this view – the Prince of Wales, who was popular with both the troops at the front and the public at home. When in January 1916 Ware set up the National Committee for the Care of Soldiers' Graves, it was the Prince who became its first President. The fear of commercialization was also expunged when the Government declared that Treasury funds would be made available to maintain the graves. Commonwealth troops were to be included in the process and the remit was cast wider than just the Western Front. In the light of all this, Ware was promoted to lieutenant colonel and given a staff of 700; his unit underwent another name change to become the Directorate of Registration and Enquiries. It was now May 1916 and his duties took the newly-titled Director-General away from the battlefields and to new offices in London. There was fresh determination now that the organization could do fine work. They could not have known at that date just how much more killing was still to come.

As more burials took place – each under individual markers, even the unknowns – the workload increased and Ware saw that more official help would be needed. He had in mind a Royal Charter to guarantee sufficient funding and staffing levels with backing throughout the Empire. The Prince of Wales was again invaluable in his support, and his father, King George V, had already shown great interest. The matter was discussed by the Imperial War Conference in the Spring of 1917, and on 21 May of the same year the King signed the document granting the Charter and the Imperial War

Graves Commission came into being, with the Prince of Wales as President and the now Brigadier-General Ware as vice-chairman.

Everyone was well aware, however, that this was just the beginning. The real work would begin when the war ended. Even as the Armistice was signed 600,000 graves had already been registered. True, many of the cemeteries were less than beautiful due to the nature of the battlefields, but with peace came the chance to make them worthy of the sacrifice they represented. The bereaved would soon want to visit their loved ones. But what of the missing? There were some 500,000 of those. It was going to be a mammoth task. Just as the French had tried to present a visual picture of their loss in the *Bilan de la Guerre*, so too did the British, using the same image of the marching dead as a single column. Four abreast, as the first passed the newly-erected Cenotaph in London, the last would be leaving Durham. It would take the entire procession three and a half days or eighty-four hours to pass. The last of the commemorations was not completed until 1938.

Work started on the cemeteries first since these already existed. Consolidation and enlargement took place, headstones being erected to both named and unknown men with no distinction as to race, class, rank or creed. A Cross of Sacrifice with a downturned sword set into it was put up in cemeteries with over 40 graves, and a non-denominational Stone of Remembrance was placed in those with over 400. Incredibly, the cemeteries were almost all complete by the mid-1920s and the task then turned to commemorating the lost. It was decided that their names would be inscribed on 'Memorials to the Missing' close to where the men had fallen. The scale of the task was huge and some of the memorials proved to be huge too. First to be unveiled was the Menin Gate in Ypres, where one in four of British war dead fell. Though massive and with space for 55,000 names, it was just the start. When it was officially opened in the summer of 1927 most thought it apt and fitting. Former Second Army Commander, General Plumer, now heading an old comrades' association called the Ypres League, spoke for many when he declared that they could now say of their loved ones: 'They are not missing. They are here.' One dissenting voice was Siegfried Sassoon, who had won a Military Cross in the war but became one of its fiercest critics. He was at the ceremony but sickened by it all. In a poem written afterwards called *On Passing the New Menin Gate* he talks of 'the intolerably nameless names' on 'this sepulchre of crime'. A similar feeling was expressed by the writer Vera Brittain when she visited the largest of all the Great War memorials to the missing, Thiepval on the Somme with its 73,000 names, shortly after its opening in 1932. She had lost everyone dear to her in the war: her brother, her fiancé and two close friends.

As anyone who has ever visited a war cemetery can testify, they are beautiful places. The remit that they should resemble English country gardens, with manicured grass and neatly tended flowerbeds, was fully met. But their creation was hard and gruesome. Many graves were transferred from isolated spots and smaller cemeteries were consolidated into larger ones – which of course meant exhuming and moving bodies. The battlefields were swept for bodies, using a grid system to make the search as thorough as possible. A minimum of six sweeps were made. Telltale signs included equipment lying around or places where the grass was lusher. In likely spots rods were inserted into the ground then sniffed for the smell of putrefaction. It was a grisly job, carried out by the Army at first but inevitably involving Commission staff also. And it was all carried out in a devastated landscape. A tale was told to one of the authors on a battlefield tour by a passenger of how his grandfather had been a newly commissioned officer sent out from Britain on this work; on arrival he was told by a senior colleague to make sure the men did the work but to supervise them lightly and not be too harsh on them. He heeded the order and soon understood it, seeing the grisly tasks the men undertook. At the end of their day's work they would seek solace in alcohol and drink to forget.

A key role in all this work would be played by the gardeners, and they were well to the fore even as the formal cemeteries were coming into being. Despite the terrible conditions the work went on at a good rate; by early 1920 the Commission already employed over 750 men and was aware that this could grow to as many as 1,500 within six months. As late as May 1919 there had only been half a dozen gardeners on the staff so a major expansion was going to be needed. Despite protests by the Treasury that local labour would be easier to find and cheaper, Ware was keen that the work should be carried out by British staff and, as in most previous cases, his view prevailed.

He was helped in this by the fact that French industry and agriculture required all available manpower for its own needs. Ware also saw a chance to help ex-servicemen, who he believed would want to do the best for their fallen comrades and would also be able to cope with the harsh conditions they would face.

By May 1920 there were over 400 gardeners in the Commission and 20 more were joining every week. One of them was David Cruickshank, who joined that July. Working in teams, most of the men bunked together, although some were billeted with local families. David had an advantage here as he was already married to a local girl and lived in Le Cateau. There would be other marriages between British gardeners and French and Belgian girls, and mixed, bilingual families emerged. Ypres even opened a school for these children so they could have a British education, and the legacy of these days still exists. One of the authors out walking with friends one day found human remains on the Somme and called in the Commission; a few days later he was asked to a meeting at the site with a staff member called Richard Moss. Hearing the name, he expected to meet a fellow Briton, and many indeed do work for the Commission. However, on arrival, the only thing Monsieur Moss was missing was a beret, a striped jersey and a string of onions! He proudly explained that his English grandfather had served in the British Army, had stayed in France after the war and married a local girl and that he was now the third generation of the family to work for the Commission.

The number of gardeners had grown to 1,362 by the following March; of these, 876 were classed as supervisors and 10 had trained at Kew Gardens. It was hard work and could involve periods away from home or based at isolated cemeteries. Travelling was still not easy over damaged or non-existent roads. But the Army's spirit of comradeship and service stood them in good stead and the men jovially called themselves 'travelling circuses' or 'travelling garden parties' as they set off to work. Typically, in these early days, a team were transported in a couple of lorries for the men and their gear, which included everything needed for the week. As well as tools, seeds and plants, they took tents, bedding, cooking kit and supplies and someone whose role would be to feed them. Clearly, as well as gardeners, there were also other workers on board such as cooks and carpenters. There was an element of the Wild West about it and the ex-soldiers were often armed – not for fear of any lingering enemy, but in the chance of bagging a rabbit or bird for the pot.

Even if a gardener was locally based he could still have a long journey to work. Many undertook lengthy daily walks there and back carrying their tools, until local contractors built sheds on site. Despite the aim to try and use exclusively British labour, the rules were bent and some locals were set on where needed. Luckier men might be equipped with an ex-Army bike, which came complete with an oil-burning lamp – although their luck was open to debate as they rode over the bone-shaking roads and tracks, and the lamp, with typical military humour, was soon christened 'the demon' for its propensity to set fire to the front wheel! Despite their status as gardeners, all shared the work of navvying – digging, levelling, shifting earth, uprooting trees. It was not without danger since there was still unexploded ordnance everywhere, and as they worked on the cemeteries some would find themselves burying the dead.

Rudyard Kipling, still closely involved with the Commission, called its task, 'The biggest single piece of work since any of the Pharaohs – and they only worked in their own country.' Work had initially concentrated on the former rear base and hospital areas, as these had good and already established transport links to carry heavy materials like bricks and stone. Great consideration had been given to the format of the grave markers, and it was quickly decided they would be a standard 2ft 6ins high and 1ft 3ins across. Portland stone was chiefly chosen as being British, plentiful and relatively cheap. As well as name and rank, it was decided that they would carry regimental crests; this initially caused problems because they all had to be carved by hand, but a machine was invented which speeded things up. A mere handful of completed stones were crossing the Channel every week in 1920, but three years later it was over 4,000. They were set into buried concrete beams to fix them at a regular height and pattern.

The key element of the gardeners' role would be horticultural, but even this was a problem initially. Flowers, plants and shrubs were simply not available on the scale needed. Seeds took time to produce for flowers as well as grass. Nurseries had been established in 1917 but three of the four set up had been destroyed in the German Spring

Offensive of 1918. The initial wartime cemeteries had used wild flowers such as poppies, cornflowers, camomile and charlock, which gave colour and even entered the public consciousness of remembrance. But the Commission wanted better, and though stocks were at first limited, there was planting of dwarf lupins, nasturtiums and others. Roses were particularly valued for their association with home, and the aim was to plant one between every two stones to cast shade as well as giving colour and scent. Hedges of beech, hornbeam and thorn formed boundaries, and quick-growing poplar and lime were mixed with slower species such as cedar for changes of proportion and colour. By spring 1921 David and his colleagues had been responsible for establishing seven nurseries, planting almost 1,000 cemeteries, laying over 15 miles of hedging, establishing 75 miles of borders with flowers and some 200 acres of lawn. Visitors were starting to arrive and the aim was to please them. Kipling wrote of visiting Rouen in 1920 on a tour covering 1,500 miles of the old war zones and thirty of its new cemeteries. He noted 'The extraordinary beauty of the cemetery and the great care that the attendants had taken of it, and the almost heartbroken thankfulness of the relatives of the dead who are there'. And he should have known, as he still clung to the hope that his only son John's body would be found and brought to such a loving environment.

Certainly pleased was a *Times* reporter who saw the first template cemetery in September 1920. He called it:

The most perfect, the noblest, the most classically beautiful memorial that any loving heart or any proud nation could desire to their fallen heroes fallen in a foreign land. Picture this strangely stirring place. A lawn enclosed of clipped turf, banded across with line on line of flowers, and linked by these bands of flowers, un-crowded, at stately intervals stand in soldierly ranks the white headstones. And while they form as perfect, as orderly a whole as any regiment on parade, yet they do not shoulder each other. Every one is set apart in flowers, every one casts its shade upon a gracious space of green. Each one, so stern in outline, is most rich in surface, for the crest of the regiment stands out with bold and arresting distinction above the strongly incised names . . . It is the grandest place I ever saw.

In May 1922 King George V and his wife, Queen Mary, made a pilgrimage to France and Flanders, together with the former Army and Navy chiefs, Earl (Douglas) Haig and Earl (David) Beatty. This party, too, had been touched by the war. In the same Ypres cemetery lay His Royal Highness Prince Maurice Battenberg, a member of the Royal Family, and Haig's brother-in-law, Charles Sackville Pelham, Lord Worsley, both regular officers killed in 1914. At Tyne Cot, destined to become the largest Commonwealth war cemetery, the King climbed a German bunker in the still evolving location and suggested it would make a fitting place for the Cross of Sacrifice, which would eventually stand there. In a speech he said he hoped the cemeteries might prevent future wars:

> In the course of my pilgrimage, I have many times asked myself whether there can be more potent advocates of peace upon earth . . . than this massed multitude of silent witnesses to the desolation of war.

He was not alone in hoping that the loss and suffering would at least be justified by this having been the 'war to end all wars'. At Etaples cemetery an incident showed that the King knew who really mattered when he produced from his pocket an envelope and asked one of the gardeners to take him to a specific grave. The envelope contained a small bunch of forget-me-nots which had been sent in a letter to Queen Mary by a mother with the request that they might be placed on her son's grave. The King bent low and carried out her wish.

David's career with the Commission began on 5 July 1920 and he was classified as a gardener, although there was far more to the job than that in those early days, as has been seen. He was now a family man as he and Aimée now had a child, a son who was named after his father. The job and regular wages were no doubt welcome, but the work was hard and perhaps brought back many bad memories, even though David was one of the lucky ones. It did also mean time apart from his new family when he had already spent so much time away from Aimée. Whatever the reason, David's career with the Commission was to prove a relatively short one and CWGC records state he left their employ on 3 April 1923. No reasons are noted and no further information is given. A family story has it that certain rule changes regarding foreigners working in France came into play at this time which meant he had to leave, but there is no hard evidence to back this up. Interestingly, in the May 1927 edition of the regimental magazine of the Cameronians, *The Covenanter*, David is described as working as a gardener, though in very poor health.

Perhaps the work did not suit his temperament. One might have thought he had already had enough excitement to last for many lifetimes and he now had family responsibilities, but it seems the still youthful David chafed at routine. He was also a city boy at heart and, coming from Glasgow as he did, perhaps found Le Cateau a little dull. It was a relatively small, insular place and one full of memories, and there must have been awkward times when he saw members of the Baudhuin family in the street going about their business. There were discussions with Aimée; David felt that he had to get away and, as his dutiful wife, she agreed. One possibility was a return to Scotland, but Aimée was not really too keen on this idea and so the decision was made to relocate to another part of France.

It is a shame that so little documentary evidence of this next part of the couple's life has come to light; all we have to go on is what has been passed down through the family. As such, there is little reason to disbelieve it, but family memory has rarely proved to be a hundred per cent reliable – even if the tale was accurately told in the first place – and we have seen that David was not beyond a little 'embellishment' when and where he felt the need. In any case, family legend has it that the Cruikshanks moved to Paris, where they took on a café – whether bought outright or leased is unknown. It would have been a tough job for a woman with a young child – and with another soon to be on the way – but not impossible. One wonderful story from this part of their life is that David acquired a 'pet' lion cub as a further attraction in the café but that Aimée was never enamoured of the unfortunate creature after it set about shredding her curtains! Whatever the circumstances of this new business venture, it did not prove a success. A further insight from later generations was that David proved a little too open to temptation by the stock, and whatever profit may have been made was soon swallowed, in his case literally.

It seems that David now put his foot down and 'suggested' that since he had tried to live in France it was Aimée's turn to give his homeland a chance; and so the next move the family made was to Glasgow. It was here that their second son was born and his parents, keen to show off his proud Gallic ancestry, gave him the name 'Georges' in the French style. The baby was christened into the Church of Scotland, whereas his four-year-old brother had been baptised in Le Cateau into the Catholic faith. One Glasgow tale is that David was walking down a street with the boys when he saw a drayman mistreating his horse by hitting it with a shovel. He grabbed the shovel from the man and gave him a beating instead. One animal he did retain some animosity against was the cat, supposedly based on his time in a German prison whose governor had a fat feline. David allegedly ate it!

It seems, however, that life in Glasgow proved little easier than in either Le Cateau or Paris, with the added problem that Aimée simply hated the city and their time there. The timing of the period in Glasgow is hazy, but the next known fact is that the family made a move again, this time south to England, where they settled at Stroud in Gloucestershire. Perhaps the draw of the location was that Aimée was a skilled weaver and the town was the home of Strachans, a well-established textile business. In fact, the area had been engaged in this trade since medieval times and the industrial revolution had brought it great prosperity. A famed local product was the so-called 'Stroud Scarlet', the high quality woollen fabric woven for the dress uniform of the Brigade of Guards. One wonders if it ever made David reflect on his own time in uniform. In time, David was also to find employment with Strachans, working as a fitter. The family settled happily in Stroud after several moves and finally put down deeper roots by taking out a mortgage on a small cottage in nearby Cainscross which was to remain their home for the rest of their married life.

Chapter 13

Courage Rewarded

So the years rolled on and everyone began to settle into their new post-war lives – some more easily than others, no doubt. While for David and Aimée these years saw several changes of domicile as they moved from France to Scotland and then England, the horizon of the French wartime heroines was obviously more restricted, through lack of money and opportunity, and they stayed in their home areas. They faced constant reminders of the war, still living as they did in devastated areas and with loved ones missing from their homes. It was true that their wartime efforts had been acknowledged by the award of a medal from the British government recognizing their aid to British soldiers, but gradually life became once more a question of looking to the future rather than dwelling too much on the past. However, in 1927 the past was about to revisit these brave, steadfast and stoical women, in a way none of them would ever have been able to imagine and with an incredible outcome. At the root of it, perhaps not surprisingly, was a former soldier.

Edward Louis Spears' background and life were extremely different to those of these simple peasant women. But they did share the country of their birth, since Spears had been born in Paris on 7 August 1886, the first child and only son of businessman Charles and his wife Marguerite (the family name was originally Spiers, but Edward changed it formally in 1918). They were wealthy, but life was not easy for the young Edward (or Louis, as he preferred his friends to call him) since his parents separated when he was young and he then suffered from typhoid and diphtheria and remained generally weak. Travel was very much a feature of his early life, with trips to visit his extended family in Ireland, other parts of France and Switzerland for the healthier air, as well as two years in a German boarding school which improved his health, physique and already considerable foreign language skills.

In 1903 he became a part-time soldier in Kildare with the Royal

Dublin Fusiliers, and this was to be the start of an exalted army career. Three years later he was commissioned as a regular in the 8th Royal Irish Hussars. He was not a typically exuberant young subaltern and did not fit easily into the messing system, preferring solitude, possessing a sometimes argumentative edge and having a scholarly air about him (he translated French military texts into English). The latter talent soon caught the attention of the Army hierarchy and in 1911 he was posted to the War Office in London, where he worked on Anglo-French codes. In early 1914 he was attached to the French Ministry of War in Paris, from where on the conflict's outbreak in August he was ordered to the front. Indeed, it was his proud boast that he considered himself to have been the first British officer to reach it.

In an age when there was much mutual misunderstanding (and often mistrust) between the British and French, Spears was a natural choice as a liaison officer, interpreting and trying to smooth ruffled national sensibilities. It was a role he performed well and it brought him swift promotion from a relatively lowly subaltern's rank to Brigadier-General in three years, as well as the opportunity of meeting everyone who was anyone in the conflict. But it would be wrong to think that he had an 'easy' time, for he was wounded four times and saw much of the human distress and disaster of war in its early days: lost comrades, shattered units and refugees fleeing for their lives with what little they could carry. Indeed, he very nearly shared the fate of many who were cut off in the confusion of early battle and captured. In his autobiography *The Picnic Basket* published in 1967 he recalled 'finding myself in a French car together with two French soldiers in the unpleasant necessity of having to drive through some German cavalry who had annoyingly wandered on to the road we had to follow on our return journey'. He put his lucky escape down to the 'bewildered Uhlans' having almost too much choice of weaponry with which to stop them! They 'fingered one weapon then another without using any as we sped past,' he wrote.

The paths of Spears and David Cruickshank could just possibly have crossed in 1914 as the officer was actually in Le Cateau before the battle in August, liaising between the British and French forces when it was the headquarters of the BEF. He described it in his book *Liaison 1914*, written in 1930, as a sleepy little town, unaware of its coming place in history.

Spears enjoyed a wartime romance with a married American heiress and writer called Mary Borden, who had set up and was running a military hospital. It was mutual attraction as soon as they met in early 1917, and an affair soon followed. After her divorce she married Spears in the French capital in January 1918. The marriage brought Spears financial security (though this faded in the Great Crash and Depression of the late 1920s and early 1930s), and following the completion of his duties as head of the British Military Mission working on the Versailles Peace Treaty he resigned his commission in June 1919. Thereafter he would follow a life of business interests and politics, twice becoming a Conservative MP, in 1922–5 and again in 1931–45. He kept up his strong French connections and was jokingly dubbed in the House of Commons 'the honourable Member for Paris.'

There were many trips across the Channel for both business and pleasure, and as a result of his former military experience Spears was also much in demand as a writer and a leader of tours of the battlefields. He had already made contact with two of the French heroines, having written to Mme Belmont-Gobert and Angèle shortly after the war, at which time the officers of the 11th Hussars sent a gift in the form of a clock bearing an engraved plate thanking them for the assistance given to one of their own regimental family.

Early in 1927 Spears was leading a military tour of the old battlefields which included a visit to Le Cateau. As he travelled from place to place he conversed with a number of people who told him of their hardships during the years of occupation. Many of the towns and villages still showed the scars of battle, and though there had been much rebuilding there was still much more to do. Some small prefabricated houses, perhaps better described as huts, had been constructed to provide much needed accommodation for families whose homes had been destroyed by artillery during the final British advance in 1918; but whilst these buildings were adequate they were cramped and offered only very basic facilities.

As Spears surveyed the remains of the damage and the new construction he was reminded by one of the party of the plight of local women who had assisted British soldiers. On making further enquiries he found that these women were now living in the direst of straits. Mme Belmont-Gobert and Angèle were still in Bertry, while

Mme Cardon had moved from there into one of the prefabricated hutments on the Rue de Peronne in Le Cateau and was working in a factory in the town. Mme Baudhuin was still resident in Le Cateau, though the house in which she had bravely protected Private Cruickshank was one of those that had been completely destroyed by shellfire in 1918.

All four women had suffered greatly during the war. Mme Belmont-Gobert had managed to keep Patrick Fowler out of the clutches of the invaders, and her daughter Angèle had made what money she could to help to feed him by creating and selling handmade embroidery work. But there was not much comfort in their lives now. Spears had been aware of her case and had once already taken it up with the authorities. He wrote:

> Hearing that she was in dire poverty, I laid the case before the War Office. This appeal led to a great deal of cogitation and scratching of heads . . . There was much goodwill, fettered unfortunately by red tape. The answer when it finally came was . . . there was no precedent for the case . . . no regulation met her case, consequently no payment could be made.

But a neat solution was applied:

> On the other hand, in somewhat irregular circumstances . . . Fowler might be said to have been billeted on her for four years. In spite of the distressing anomaly that the only properly constituted authority . . . had been German, and that therefore the correct return had not been made at the right time, a point was stretched, and it was ruled that Madame Belmont-Gobert was entitled to Fowler's extra messing allowance at the rate of 2d [two pence] a day, and that the requisite forms might be dispensed with.

So the sum of 2,043 francs 50 centimes was duly sent to Mme Belmont-Gobert, and the War Office also informed the King, who awarded the Order of the British Empire to both her and Angèle. These were generous gestures and might have helped, had not the scrupulously honest woman used the bulk of the money to pay off outstanding debts to friends built up during the war; it was soon all gone and she was in trouble again. On receiving news of her plight a second time, the regiment sent her a further sum, and the actions of the British prompted the French authorities to recognize her situation and award her a small pension.

By now Mme Cardon was a widow as her husband had never really recovered from his wartime experiences and had died shortly after the war's end. Spears describes her in 1927 as living in little more than a hovel and in extreme poverty. Both she and Gabrielle, who was fourteen, were now working long hours in a local factory, and life was tough. There were also two other children in the family. Spears revealed that the grieving parents of Corporal Herbert Hull had offered to adopt one of the youngsters at the end of the war, but 'the indomitable mother determined that while she had strength she would bring up her family, and the offer was gratefully refused'.

Mme Baudhuin, who had been reunited with her POW husband Jules at the end of the war, had, like Mme Cardon, suffered harsh treatment in German prisons, and both women continued to suffer from poor health as a consequence. They had both been awarded the bronze Allied Subjects Medal by the British government, little recognition for their heroic acts and for what they had suffered in providing succour and safety to British soldiers in desperate need, but appreciated all the same. The years after their release had been hard and things did not look like getting any better; poverty was common to all and it was a case of the poor looking after their neighbours as best they could.

Spears was saddened by their situation and immediately decided that the heroic actions of these ladies and their current plight constituted a story that the British public should be made aware of. He therefore decided to use his connections in society and wrote to the owner of the *Daily Telegraph*, Viscount Burnham, to ask if their brave wartime deeds and current peacetime difficulties could be publicized in his newspaper. Burnham was a pillar of the establishment and the community, having had a wide and varied career including spells as a Member of Parliament, a barrister, a London county councillor and Mayor of Stepney, and including war service commanding a battalion of the Royal Buckinghamshire Yeomanry. He had become the *Telegraph*'s managing proprietor in

January 1916, been created a viscount in 1919 and after the war continued to be active in heading various charities.

Burnham was greatly moved by what he heard and immediately agreed to do what he could, commissioning the journalist Herbert Walton to travel to France to meet the four women from Le Cateau and Bertry, as well as others who had been involved, and record their stories at first hand. Sadly, there were many who could not be interviewed as they had paid the ultimate price for their humane actions in helping those desperate soldiers in their time of greatest need. The war memorials in Le Cateau, Bertry and other nearby towns bear witness to the loss of civilian lives during the period of occupation in the area.

Walton did not hang about and his first report appeared in the *Telegraph* on 14 February 1927 telling the story of Trooper Fowler and his saviours Mme Belmont-Gobert and Angèle. Incredibly, it was a story which had never before been told to the public.

The response from the readership was immediate and overwhelming. On the same day as the article appeared, a letter was received by the newspaper which was published with the second instalment of the story which ran the next day. It was printed under the headline 'Offer of Help' and read:

> To the Editor of the *Daily Telegraph*.
> Sir – with reference to the most touching and stirring account in your issue of today of the long-endured heroism of Mme Belmont-Gobert. I venture to suggest that a 'Rente-viagère' (life annuity) assuring the comfort of her remaining years, would be the most appropriate method of showing our deep and reverent admiration. If you should think well of this idea I shall rejoice to subscribe 250 francs, and I think I shall be only one of many.
> Yours. F. H. C.
> London. Feb. 14th.

The *Telegraph*'s editorial staff knew a good story when they saw one, so seized the idea and replied:

> We are prepared to receive any subscriptions that may be sent for Madam Belmont-Gobert, and to see that they are applied to her assistance.

And so it began. By the first post on the morning of 15 February letters of support were being received by the newspaper together with donations from readers who were moved by the story of Trooper Fowler and the post-war plight of his saviours. Four further letters were printed on 16 February, one of which read:

> Sir,
> I read your account of Mme Belmont-Gobert this morning with great interest. I feel convinced that a large number of your readers who did so will feel great disappointment if they are not offered an opportunity of showing in a practical manner their admiration for this French lady's noble self-sacrifice. In the hope that it may induce you to open a subscription list, I enclose my cheque.
> Yours. B. Grey.
> Farningham.

On 17 February the newspaper printed the story of Corporal Herbert Hull and his protectors, the Cardon family. Further letters of support from readers accompanied the report, together with a list of the names of donors. Additional offerings had been received by Brigadier-General Spears. The donations ranged in value from two shillings (10p in the decimal system) sent in by M. W. F. of Broadstone to £50 received from a Frank Lloyd. One of the donations, of two shillings and sixpence, was given by a man who signed himself 'An Ex-service Tommy'. Donations were also being received in French francs and ranged from 10 francs from 'A Padre' in Reading, to 500 francs offered by 'J. C.' of Westcliff-on-Sea. The total received to date amounted to £126 and 19 shillings.

It was the issue of 18 February which carried the amazing tale of David Cruickshank and his protectors Julie-Celestine Baudhuin and her family; by now the British public was well and truly hooked and the money was flowing in a torrent, to the extent that it was reported in the 19 February edition that a staggering £494 13s 6d had by now come in to the newspaper in the form of donations large, small and everything in between.

As the fund grew it was decided that, as had been suggested, annuities should be purchased to provide a lasting income for each of these brave women; but it was felt that even more could and should be done by the *Telegraph* to show the appreciation of the whole nation to these French heroines. Simply providing them with a pension was not felt sufficient to reflect the feelings of the readers. It was therefore proposed that they should be invited, as guests of the newspaper, to travel to London, where with great ceremony they would then be presented with their annuities by the Lord Mayor of London at the Mansion House. When plans for this presentation were drawn up and the event publicized there was a tremendous demand for tickets; it seemed that the whole of the *Telegraph*'s readership wanted to attend, to see these French heroines for themselves and show the ladies their appreciation.

Events now moved quickly. At 0800 hrs on a dull April morning the Frenchwomen left their homes in Bertry and Le Cateau on a journey that would take them to the heart of the great British Empire. Mme Belmont-Gobert travelled with her daughter, now Mme Angèle Lesur, Mme Cardon was accompanied by her daughter Gabrielle and Mme Baudhuin by her husband Jules. The Mayors of Le Cateau and Bertry, M Lebeau and M Bracq, together with their wives, had also been invited and led the party. None of the women had any experience of foreign travel other than to and from the German prisons in which they had been incarcerated, and certainly none had ever travelled by sea. They were simple small town working folk with no experience of anything other than getting by in their difficult daily lives.

After travelling by train via Lille and Calais, the group had a choppy ferry crossing of the Channel before being met on their arrival at Dover by four officers and four non-commissioned officers of the 11th Hussars from Shorncliffe. It was this regiment to which both Corporal Hull and Trooper Fowler had belonged. Captain P. G. Rivière and those with him expressed the debt the regiment owed to these Frenchwomen who had done so much for their comrades at such great cost. The party arrived at London's Victoria station at approximately 1830 hrs and were received on behalf of the newspaper by Lieutenant Colonel E. F. Lawson. Speaking for Viscount Burnham, he extended to the heroines and their party a most hearty welcome. In return, M Lebeau and M

Bracq expressed the privilege they felt at accompanying these brave and noble women to England. Amongst those attending this informal ceremony were members of the Associations of Great Britain and France. A touching incident was the meeting of Mme Belmont-Gobert and her sister Mme Helene Georges, who lived in London; they had not seen each other for twelve years. On the drive to their hotel the visitors were amazed at the capital's traffic. 'Mais c'est épatant [it's amazing]', they kept saying. They gazed with reverence at the statue of Nurse Edith Cavell, who was tried and executed by the Germans for helping escapee soldiers and whose name reminded them of their own sufferings. M Lebeau expressed his pleasure at the warmth of their reception, saying, 'Our visit will, I am convinced, be a memorable event in the history of Anglo-French relations.'

Printed in the newspaper on the following morning was the full programme for that day. This group from rural France was going to get the best VIP treatment that the great capital city at the heart of the British Empire could provide. The programme for the day is reproduced below as it appeared in the *Telegraph*:

An interesting programme has been arranged for the party's entertainment today by the Welcome Committee of the United Association of Great Britain and France, on whose behalf Lady (Ian) Malcolm, the chairman, and Miss Olive Maxse, the hon. secretary, will call at the heroines' hotel this morning. A visit to the Tower of London, where Colonel Dan Burges VC, the resident Governor, will welcome the party, will be followed by lunch with Lady Malcolm. In the afternoon Mr Wilson, Clerk of the Works at the Houses of Parliament, will conduct a tour of both houses and the Crypt, and Canon Foxley Norris will subsequently render a similar service at Westminster Abbey. Tea will be taken at Chelsea Hospital with the Hon. Lady Littleton.

It was an illustrious group with whom to spend the day, and although much of their fame would no doubt have been lost on their French guests, they would have been impressed by their hosts' manners and kindness. Lady Malcolm was the daughter of the well known Victorian actress Lillie Langtry, who had had a scandalous three-year affair with the then Prince of Wales, the future King Edward VII. There were also strong rumours that another royal prince – Louis von Battenberg – was Lady Malcolm's father! Canon Foxley Norris had painful and still recent memories of the war, as his son John had been wounded serving as a major and had finally succumbed to his injuries in 1924. Miss Maxse's brother, Ivor, had been one of the most successful generals of the war and had risen to become the Army's chief instructor by its end. Lady Littleton's family had also paid a price in the war: she had lost a nephew, Lieutenant Neil Shaw Stewart aged twenty-two, on the Somme in 1916.

How these simple Frenchwomen and their party must have wondered at the sights of London, having left their still battle-scarred towns a mere twenty-four hours earlier. How strange it must have been for them to be feted by members of the British aristocracy in such lavish style and how wonderful to be waited upon in surroundings so very different to those to which they were accustomed. We can only speculate as to the excited conversation when they returned to their hotel after such a marvellous day. Whatever they were feeling at the end of their first full day in the capital, they could have had no perception of what was to follow in the days to come. It was to exceed their wildest dreams.

And still the money kept flooding in to the *Telegraph*, so that on the following morning, 9 April, the newspaper could report that the total amount received into their fund for the heroines had reached £3,108 – a considerable sum in 1927, representing approximately £150,000 at the time of writing (2015). The cost of the visit and all expenses were being covered by the newspaper, so every penny donated by their readers was going to support the women. The annuities thus purchased would provide a welcome source of income which would help to lift the four women from the depth of poverty they had endured for so many years. Apart from the £300 donated by the *Telegraph* itself, the largest single donation was £50 and the smallest 4d (four pence). Many messages of support had been received, including one from a young girl known only as Joan who sent in five shillings 'for the brave Frenchies'.

On the same day the newspaper also reported:

Every ticket for today's meeting at the Mansion House was allocated on Wednesday. The proceedings, which will take place in the famous Egyptian Hall, are timed to begin at noon, but from 11.30 a.m. selections of music will be given by the band of the Honourable Artillery Company. Ticket holders are advised to be in their place early.

The hall, with a capacity for 350 seated guests, was renowned as one of the most splendid in London. Despite its name, it has no Egyptian decoration but its interior was based on designs by the classical Roman architect Vitruvius of buildings in Egypt, with giant columns supporting a narrower attic area. Marble statues dating from 1854–64 stand between the columns, and the magnificent stained glass was installed in 1868.

There would have been great excitement for the women and their party as they made themselves ready for their journey to the Mansion House that Saturday morning, for they were to be the centre of attention and meet the Lord Mayor of London, who was to present them with gifts in recognition and appreciation of their great deeds during the dark period of the Great War. How the memories must have flooded back. It had been only a few months since they had been interviewed by the *Telegraph* reporter, but nine difficult years had passed since the enemy had been driven from the streets of their towns, during which they had done their best to re-make a life for themselves and their families.

Despite the surroundings, the ceremony must have brought reminders of their suffering. The Baudhuin family had been torn apart by the war: Julie-Celestine's husband Jules taken as a POW during 1914, her son Léon sentenced to hard labour in a German logging camp far from home, her only daughter, still in her mind a baby though aged fourteen, left alone and thrown on the mercy of neighbours after her mother was transported to Siegburg prison, and her firstborn, Jules, killed in action defending his country from the invaders. Her life had been ripped apart, and she had risked her own neck as she stood up to beg the German tribunal not to execute her 'adopted Scottish son' David Cruickshank. But while her husband had returned from the war and her son from his enforced labour imposed by the enemy, and she had tried to rebuild her life as best she could, Julie-Celestine bore another sadness which her trip to Britain must have brought into sharp focus again. David, the youthful Cameronian soldier she had done so much for, was alive and well, but the rift that had developed between them, so severe that it had torn them apart shortly after the war, had never been mended. In a number of post-war interviews David made no mention of the heroic plea made by Julie-Celestine to the military tribunal that undoubtedly saved him from the firing squad. David was most conspicuous by his absence in all these London proceedings, and at no point was he mentioned by name. Others closely involved had been invited and were present. It is not known whether he was invited or whether Julie-Celestine had asked that he should not attend. Or perhaps he was invited but declined. It was a great shame, all the same, and perhaps a golden opportunity to heal the rift had been lost.

Mme Cardon's family, too, had suffered tremendously. Her husband was not long dead, having never truly recovered from the exertions, hardships and strain of surviving while hiding in the woods from the Germans after Private Hull had been captured at their home. Her British fugitive had been cruelly ill treated before his execution. Her children had also been left alone when she was betrayed and thrown into prison. Her youngest daughter, Gabrielle, was now fourteen years of age but remained weak and sickly as a result of the deprivations of the war years.

Mme Belmont-Gobert and her daughter Angèle Lesur had spent three years and nine months protecting Trooper Patrick Fowler, who now made the journey down from his home in Scotland and was with them during most of their time in London. It must have been a very emotional reunion for them all. They must have prayed many times to the saints who watched over them during those terrifying years of fear and privation, but now, on this day, their deeds were finally to be acknowledged.

On a day as auspicious as this one not a single moment was to be wasted, and so in the morning before attending the ceremony at the Mansion House they were taken on a tour of London Zoo. Then it was on to the Mansion House for the main event, and the party was met there by a huge crowd of well-wishers, all eager to meet these French heroines and thank them in person for their brave deeds.

The *Telegraph*'s report of it all appeared the following day:

Madame Belmont-Gobert, Madame Angèle Lesur, Madame
Louise Cardon and Madame Julie Baudhuin – their names
should live forever in their country's history – were yesterday
the honoured guests of the Lord Mayor of London at a
meeting such as even the Mansion House can seldom have
seen. With a distinguished company around them on the
platform and a great gathering that crowded the Egyptian Hall
to its doors in front of them, quietly they sat – four humble
figures in black, with only the glitter of a cross or medal to
relieve the sombreness of their attire.

On the platform to the right of the Lord Mayor (Sir Rowland
Blades Bt) Mme Belmont-Gobert sat next to the French
Ambassador; her daughter Mme Lesur was neighbour to
Viscount FitzAlan of Derwent, Mme Cardon and Mme Baudhuin
sat between Field Marshal Sir William Robertson and Sir Charles
Wakefield. Near them were Viscount and Viscountess Burnham,
the *Maires* of their own towns of Bertry and Le Cateau, Trooper
Fowler, Mme Baudhuin's husband Jules and Gabrielle Cardon
who was left desolate when the Germans sent her mother to
prison and her father was driven to his death. And, on duty in
their special honour were the City of London's world famous
mace and sword and the glittering figure of the City Marshal.

As well as the heroines themselves, there was an astonishing
amount of Great War history on that platform in the form of Field
Marshal Robertson and Sir Charles Wakefield. The redoubtable
'Wully' Robertson had been humbly born into a shopkeeping family
in a Lincolnshire village sixty-seven years earlier. But he chose the
Army and became (and remains) the only soldier to have risen
through every one of its ranks from private to field marshal. Between
1916 and 1918 he was Chief of the Imperial General Staff, liaising
between government and army – in effect its top soldier. Highly able,
irascible and likely to drop his aitches when excited, he was described
by Spears as 'an ambulating refrigerator' of a man. Lancashire-born
Sir Charles had made his name and fortune in engineering and had
formed the Wakefield Oil Company, later changing its name to

Castrol. After the war he had been very moved by a newspaper article by the famous wartime padre Tubby Clayton which described a recent trip to the former battlefields, lamenting that many of their features were disappearing and suggesting that some far-sighted individual or organization should step in to save things before it was too late. Sir Charles agreed and bought Talbot House in Poperinghe which Tubby had run as a much-loved refuge from the war open to both officers and other ranks, as well as the Spanbroekmolen mine crater blown on the Messines Ridge in 1917. Both are now much visited places of remembrance on the Ypres Salient.

The *Telegraph* report continued:

> If the platform held a notable assembly, the great body of the meeting was hardly less remarkable. Old men were there and boys who were still at school; women who had come from many parts of England and had been content to 'queue up' outside the Mansion House for hours; stalwart figures in khaki from the 11th Hussars – Trooper Fowler's regiment – and one sad-eyed, elderly man whose abiding sorrow could not prevent the expression of his gratitude to the woman who had tried in vain to save the life of Corporal Hull, his son, and in doing so had almost shared the poor lad's fate.
>
> All were there to acknowledge the debt that each of them felt as a personal obligation to the four modest figures on the platform, whose formal presentation to the Lord Mayor by Viscount Burnham brought the whole of this great assembly to its feet. The triple story of almost incredible heroism as repeated by the Lord Mayor, aroused in his audience an obvious emotion, which soon found relief in enthusiastic cheers. Following his speech he presented to each of the woman a certificate for the annuity purchased with the donations received from the readers of the *Daily Telegraph*. With each certificate he also presented the women with an illuminated address which recorded the intrepid courage they had shown during those dark days of occupation. The pensions earned from the donations were £60 to Madame Belmont-Gobert, £26 to Angèle, and £52 each to Madames Cardon and Baudhuin.

The illuminated scrolls which recorded the endeavours of each of the women were absolute works of art. Each was personalized to its recipient and gave a brief account of their brave and selfless actions. Interestingly, and perhaps in evidence of the depth of the rift between Julie-Celestine and David and the impossibility of its repair, he is not mentioned by name at all, although his regiment's badge is there.

Then there were a number of speeches. First to speak was the French Ambassador, followed by Lord FitzAlan of Derwent. Then Field Marshal Sir William Robertson also offered his sincere thanks to the heroines on behalf of the Army and nation; and the last speech was from Viscount Burnham, who echoed those sentiments and said it had been a privilege to help thank these women properly and give them their due deserts. As the speeches ended, the band of the Honourable Artillery Company played the French and British National Anthems.

With the formalities over, the Lord Mayor and Lady Mayoress were to entertain the French guests to lunch, but not before the heroines had received the personal congratulations of as many of the assembled company as could get near them. Those present were also anxious to see the wardrobe in which Trooper Fowler had been concealed and which was on display. Trooper Fowler's reaction on seeing this particular piece of furniture was not recorded; he most certainly would have not wanted to get inside it again!

Amidst the crowd the four simple grey-haired women in their best black dresses stood quietly and tried to take it all in. Mme Belmont-Gobert delighted in speaking the patois of their region with Trooper Fowler, who before this trip to London she had not seen for eight years; despite the passage of time, he had forgotten neither the language nor the great debt he owed this woman and her family.

Emotions must have been running high for everyone present, but now perhaps the most exceptional moment took place. An elderly man was brought forward and presented to Mme Cardon. He was Mr George Hull, father of the unfortunate Corporal Hull whom the Frenchwoman had done so much to protect. The reporter who witnessed the event wrote of it:

I saw Mr Hull take the hands of Mme Cardon. He tried for a moment to express his gratitude. He spoke in English although Mme Cardon spoke only French. But they understood one another. Why words? They were quietly, silently, thinking of the glorious dead. And suddenly the father went down on his knees and kissed the feet of the old Frenchwoman who had risked her life for the sake of his son. Tears were in all eyes.

Even after all this, the day was not yet over, for after lunch the party were the guests of the Anglo-French Luncheon Club for tea at the Princes Restaurant, and in the evening they were entertained at the Coliseum Theatre; also in the audience that night was the French national rugby team. Heroines the ladies might well be, but they would undoubtedly have been little short of exhausted after this most remarkable of days, which must have required a heroic level of stamina. Hopefully, the excitement of it all did not prevent them from sleeping, for there was another big day coming up on the morrow.

Sunday was inevitably going to be just as hectic, perhaps the most exciting day of their visit and possibly the most memorable of their lives. During their time in London, transport for the French party had been provided by friends of the United Associations of Great Britain and France, and today was no exception. They were first taken to luncheon with Viscount and Viscountess Burnham at their home, Hall Barn, set in beautiful Buckinghamshire countryside. After lunch, the cars arrived at the agreed hour and the party were soon heading for Windsor. Honoured as they had been during the events of the past three days, today was to bring to them the highest honour imaginable. Today, these humble Frenchwomen who had been living in poverty in post-war France were to be entertained to tea at Windsor Castle, after which they would be presented to their Majesties King George V and Queen Mary of England. Julie-Celestine Baudhuin and Marie-Louise Cardon proudly wore their medals bearing the King's image. Madame Belmont-Gobert and Angèle were also adorned with their OBEs. Trooper Patrick Fowler travelled with the party, for he too was to meet his sovereign. No doubt he was also wearing his best bib and tucker and his medals.

At the Castle the party was entertained to tea, with Lord Stamfordham, the King's Private Secretary, presiding at one table, and Lady Ampthill, Lady in Waiting to the Queen, at the other. It was perhaps an opportunity to attempt to calm the nerves of the guests in such exceptional circumstances. After tea and a little conversation, the four French ladies and Trooper Fowler were ushered in to be received by the King and Queen, with the Prince of Wales also in attendance. The Prince, who had served in the war and had been very popular with the troops, had been keenly interested in the scheme for bringing the French heroines to London, had insisted on being with the King and Queen at their reception and had motored down to Windsor in time for luncheon with their Majesties.

The King immediately put the Frenchwomen at their ease by talking to them in their own language, questioning them about their experiences in the war and asking Mme Belmont-Gobert and her daughter how they managed to keep Trooper Fowler concealed in a cupboard for so long. The King sympathized with Mme Cardon and Mme Baudhuin on having undergone imprisonment in Germany for the part they took in succouring British fugitives. Turning to Patrick Fowler, the King enquired how had he managed to take exercise while cooped up in his cramped hiding place, and the former trooper explained that he made occasional excursions into the fresh air while his protectors kept a vigilant lookout for the enemy. The ladies were presented with a signed photograph of the King and Queen, and his Majesty said that he hoped the souvenirs would help them to forget some of the suffering they had been through.

Afterwards the guests were all thrilled to see the baby Princess Elizabeth, born the year before and the future Queen Elizabeth II. They were also introduced to the elder son of Princess Mary and Viscount Lascelles who would later become the 7th Earl of Harewood. The Frenchwomen were totally overcome by the graciousness shown them by their royal hosts and asked that their great gratitude might be expressed to the King and Queen for their kindness.

When they got back to their hotel they were met by the press, who wanted to know how it had all gone. The heroines were unanimous in their reply: 'It has been a marvellous day,' they said, as they stood flushed and excited in the lounge of their hotel. Of the King, Mme Cardon said, 'He was very kind,' and Mme Baudhuin told a reporter, 'We could never have imagined that such a reception would be given to ordinary poor working people such as we are.' They may have been poor working people, but ordinary they most certainly were not and they thoroughly deserved every bit of the honour bestowed on them.

The following day they were to leave the city that had shown them how much the people of Great Britain appreciated their heroic deeds in putting their own and their families' lives of at risk for the sake of foreign strangers. Even the King and Queen of England and the future King, the Prince of Wales, had felt the need to meet them and to shake their hands. In their eyes no greater honour could have been bestowed upon them. Their journey back home to France and their more modest abodes was uneventful, but they must have remained astounded for quite some time afterwards by what they had experienced. And of course there was much re-living of the remarkable events as they recounted them to their families and friends. Their illuminated scrolls went on the wall, and the pensions hopefully made their lives easier and more comfortable.

Epilogue

The promise made at its end to those who had suffered so much in the Great War was that their suffering and loss had not all been in vain and that the conflict had in fact been 'the war to end wars.' It could not and never would be allowed to happen again, the politicians said. Politicians like to speak in such ringing tones, but the reality is of course often very different. The peace settlement reached by the Treaty of Versailles in Europe would in time create as many problems as it was intended to dispel, and while, theoretically at least, the new League of Nations had been created to stop or solve disputes between countries before they descended again into war, it soon proved to be a paper tiger. Three empires had fallen, spanning centuries of history in the case of the Habsburgs of Austria-Hungary and the Romanovs of Russia, as well as the more recently emerged Hohenzollerns in Germany. Russia had fallen to Communism under Lenin and it had been a close call whether Germany might not go the same way. The Bolshevik menace was felt right through the continent and beyond. In the circumstances there could only be turbulent times ahead.

While Britain and France had eventually emerged victorious, they had both been tremendously weakened in material, economic and emotional terms, and their populations had understandably had enough of war. Most of the people of the defeated states undoubtedly felt this way too. The politicians of the leading democracies seemed to realize this. But for this bright future of 'no more war' to become a reality, the leaders of all countries needed to sign up to it, and the political will of all was necessary to make it come about. Critically, America was soon to turn to isolationism after the war and wanted nothing to do with the new League of Nations. And a 'perfect storm' of events was about to engulf Europe and the world once more, with the peace treaties barely a decade old and the memorials to the war's dead still being constructed. Banking crises, economic collapse, political instability and the rise of totalitarian governments, especially that of Hitler and the Nazis, saw potential war clouds begin to gather again.

Most of the people who have appeared in this story were not involved in the higher echelons of political life and had little choice other than to live with the outcome of such great events. They were simply ordinary folk trying to get on with their lives to the best of their ability if allowed to do so. War had already exacted a heavy price from them in so many ways, and now they only hoped to be left alone to try to rebuild their lives and achieve some happiness in what was left of them. But, as before, events beginning to unfold outside their control would be the deciding factor.

While finally settling happily in Stroud, David and Aimée Cruickshank never forgot France and made frequent trips back to Le Cateau to visit members of the Olivier family and friends. These continued until 1960, when they stayed with Aimée's sister Céline and her husband, Alfred Vincent. The outbreak of the Second World War in 1939 had curtailed these trips, and it must have been a period of great worry, particularly for Aimée, and have triggered some unhappy memories for David also. There was worry for them, too, as both boys went off to serve, as did one of David's brothers with the Australian army. In May 1940 the Germans invaded again and this time conquered France. Hitler was so pleased with himself that he made the French surrender in the same railway carriage at Compiègne where Germany had been forced to sign the Armistice in November 1918, then had it taken back to the Fatherland for victory celebrations and eventual destruction. Le Cateau was again occupied by the Germans and its inhabitants endured the same privations, fears and jealousies and no doubt staged similar feats of remarkable and unseen defiance. But thankfully France survived this ordeal too.

David and Aimée in time became grandparents, and there are vivid and cherished memories of visits to their home from family members. Glen Cruickshank, their grandson, recalls:

My nanny invariably had boxes of Smarties for us children and would sing *Frère Jacques* to us. Sometimes when she spoke she would not know the English word she was looking for and would ask Grandad in French for the correct word, as his French was much better than her English. She used to call him an 'old bugger' which was one of the English phrases she had picked up! I remember her cooking beautiful food.

David had clearly also not forgotten his time as soldier:

My grandfather was a member of the Stroud branch of the British Legion, whose club was just across the road from their cottage. He would invariably go there during his lunchtime for a pint or two.

Sadly, Aimée did not live to a ripe old age; she died in 1964 after suffering a stroke while hanging out some washing. David was devastated by her death, as she had been the light of his life, and he struggled to cope without her. He found he could not stay in their home so he sold the cottage and decided to return to Glasgow. But, according to the family, the money was soon spent and so he came back again to Stroud to be with his son and family. He lived comfortably but became more reclusive in later years, staying mostly in his bedroom reading cowboy books, which he enjoyed greatly, and watching the horse racing on the television set which he kept in there. His interest in racing was more than merely a pastime, as Glen remembered:

My granddad enjoyed a flutter on the horses and often won. He had a keen brain and could tell, to the penny, exactly how much he was due back from the bookie – often before the bookie had worked it out himself.

David retained some French habits and tastes which reflected his earlier life. He enjoyed that particularly Gallic alcoholic drink of *pastis* and water, along with red wine and cognac but, true Scotsman that he was, he also enjoyed his whisky and knew his spirit – as Glen soon found out when he was sent on an errand once to buy him his favourite brand:

On one occasion I was sent to the local off-licence to buy my granddad a bottle of Teacher's whisky. Unfortunately, when I got there they had sold out of Teacher's so I bought him Bell's instead. Hoping he wouldn't notice, I poured him out a glass and took it to him. He took one look at it and, without even tasting it, said, 'I'm not drinking that!' as he knew it wasn't Teacher's.

Before a sip of whatever drink he was about to enjoy he would always offer up a jolly wish of '*bon santé*' or 'good health' to everyone assembled.

Life continued in this vein for David after Aimée's death, but it was almost as if he was really just counting the days until he could be reunited with her. He thought about her every day, and every day he saw her face, because his arm still bore the tattoo he had done himself of his then sweetheart many years before when he was longing for her in his captivity. Theirs had been a real wartime love drama, fortunately one with a happy ending, and David finally joined his beloved when he died after a short illness in July 1973 aged 78.

Patrick Fowler had been written off for dead in the war. His official Army papers recorded his death on 24 December 1915. But he had survived and emerged from his hiding place when British troops entered Bertry in October 1918. Amazingly, his old unit were among the liberators of the village, and he could not wait to make his presence known to his former comrades. Not surprisingly perhaps, when he started trying to tell his incredible tale, it was not initially believed and he was suspected by some of being a spy; he could easily have been shot out of hand, with emotions running so high. Rather than being offered congratulations he was arrested; but perhaps the most incredible bit of good fortune now occurred, one he had surely earned after his ordeal. One of the officers of the 11th Hussars was a Major Drake; remarkably, he had been Fowler's troop officer in 1914 and he recognized him and was able to verify his identity! Now his liberators were ready to hear about his ordeal and believe him.

Fowler's service papers, the same ones which recorded him going missing presumed dead, now had an addition made to them. On the very next line the entry inscribed on 29 October 1918 baldly states: 'Rejoins regiment after missing'. Talk about an understatement! He was perhaps not surprisingly in a pretty poor state, both physically and mentally (indeed, a 1906 medical had reported his physical development then as 'very poor'). Happily, he was almost immediately granted leave of a month, after which he then did have to rejoin his unit in France. But his service of nearly two decades was almost over now, and he returned to Britain on 12 January 1919 to camp at Fovant; two days short of a month later, he was listed as

Class Z, the lowest level of fitness, and demobbed. His papers also note that he was entitled to his full award of medals.

On leaving the army Fowler was offered employment as a valet by a former officer of the 11th Hussars, Major the Hon Robert Bruce, who owned the large Glenernie estate in the Highlands of Scotland. Fowler and his wife, Gertrude, settled in the village of Forres in Moray, but tragedy was to strike soon afterwards when she died giving birth to their third child in 1920. The child, a third daughter, survived and was given the middle name Angèle in memory of the younger of his saviours. 'His' wardrobe was bought by Lord Wakefield from the Belmont-Gobert family and was donated to the regimental museum, where it is still on display to the public in Winchester. In 2000 it was announced that a film was to be made of his story by producer Bill Shepherd; it was to be called *Close Quarters* and filmed at Shepperton Studios and on location in France. Funding to the tune of £3 million was said to be in place, with Robert Carlyle rumoured to be playing Fowler and the renowned French actress Jeanne Moreau as Mme Belmont-Gobert. Sadly, however, nothing came of the project. Fowler, who had come a long way since his birth in Dublin, died at the grand old age of ninety in 1964.

Mme Belmont-Gobert herself had another twenty-one years of life after her trip to London, spending some of her time living in St Quentin. Both she and Angèle lived through the Second World War but thankfully survived long enough to see peace restored. The redoubtable Marie lived on into her eighties but finally died in 1948. Angèle survived her by only twelve years, dying in 1960 in her mid-sixties, her life perhaps having been shortened by the wartime hardships, which had left her weakened. They share a gravestone in the cemetery at Bertry upon which, along with their details (incidentally, spelling their surname as 'Belmant-Gobert') there is inscribed '*héroique de France*' and the emblem of their OBEs. It clearly remained something of which they and their family were justifiably very proud.

Julie-Celestine Baudhuin remained in Le Cateau for the rest of her life. Her former house having been destroyed by British shelling at the end of the war, a new home was found for her and the family at 15 Rue Carlier. Both Julie-Celestine and her daughter Marie found work in a local textile factory. In 1926 they moved once more, this time to a new housing estate called the Cité Picard, now known as the Rue des Hirondelles. With 1936 coming to an end, and as the clouds of war started to gather again over Europe, Julie-Celestine passed away, aged sixty. It was not a great age, but again the strain and hardships of her life had perhaps shortened her span. Her funeral took place in the afternoon of 10 December, and a newspaper report recorded that a hearse left her home followed by a large crowd including the current mayor of Le Cateau, M Henri Preux, along with the former wartime deputy mayor and hero, M Emile Picard. On a cushion placed on her coffin were the three medals she had been awarded: the bronze Allied Subjects Medal from King George V, the French silver Reconnaissance Medal for wartime assistance and another medal from France's Ministry of Foreign Affairs. It is not known whether David was made aware of her death at the time, but he must have been told on one of the family's later visits.

The last of the heroines to depart was Marie-Louise Cardon, who died in 1971 aged eighty-four. She too had lived through and survived another world war. In the immediate post-war years she stayed close to the scene of her bravery and devotion. The family lived in one of the wooden temporary dwellings called 'barracks' by the locals on the Rue de Peronne-sur-Selle. Life was hard. Her husband Gustave's death aged only forty, just after the war, had left her with three children aged fifteen, fourteen and twelve. The year before, she had also been awarded the French Reconnaissance Medal, but it had no pension attached to it, which was why she and her youngest daughter, Gabrielle, worked in a local textile mill. The elder children stayed on at school thanks to the aid of neighbours and friends. She eventually moved to Faches-Thumesnil near Lille, where she died half a century after being widowed. Her death closed the final chapter of the story of those simple but steadfast women.

Dying in the same year was the man who was largely responsible for their getting some belated wider and financial acknowledgement for their sacrifice, Edward Louis Spears. Unlike their post-war struggles, Spears' return home was to a somewhat gilded life of business, politics, travel and literature, and he was comfortably off despite financial problems caused by the Great Crash and difficulties in his business ventures in Czechoslovakia later in the 1930s. He had formed a strong friendship with Churchill during the war and this was to remain a constant; the two men feared the worst when they saw Hitler and the Nazis rising to power and European and world peace threatened once again. Both urged that the policy of appeasement was the wrong tactic and that Britain should make a stand against the Nazi threat, but to begin with this was not a popular view. Spears, given his strong French links, became chairman of the Anglo-French Committee of the House of Commons, and in August 1939 he and Churchill were invited to inspect the French Maginot Line defences.

Although long retired, Spears was to serve prominently in the coming war. When Churchill became Prime Minister in May 1940 he immediately summoned Spears to Downing Street and appointed him his personal representative to the French Prime Minister and Defence Minister, Paul Reynaud. He was promoted from his retirement rank to Major General and had to look out bits of his Great War uniform to wear once more. Sent to France, he quickly renewed many acquaintances and said that Marshal Pétain treated him like a long lost son. But he feared French morale was brittle and thought the alliance with Britain was under threat. Morale plummeted further as the Germans advanced, and Paris was declared an open city to save it from destruction. It fell on 14 June and Pétain, France's new Prime Minister, now saw no other option than an armistice. The government had fled to Bordeaux and Spears had to try and save what he could from the situation. Fearing arrest, he managed to get de Gaulle away on a plane to London. On landing, the future leader of the Free French government based in the British capital gave Spears a signed photograph made out to 'General Spears. Witness, ally, friend'. Sadly, their friendship did not endure.

Until 1942 Spears headed the British Mission to the Free French Government and was then appointed Minister to Syria and Lebanon. To this day there is a street named after him in Beirut! During the war his wife was very active, too, and re-established her medical unit which had operated throughout the Great War tending the French wounded. It served with the Free French forces in campaigns through the Middle East, North Africa, Italy and France itself and was allowed to take part in the Victory Parade in Paris in June 1945, when British forces were not. But de Gaulle seemingly disapproved of the unit displaying the Union Flag alongside the French national Tricolour, despite fervent cheers from the crowds, and had its British members sent home afterwards, much to the anger of Spears and his wife. They protested, but to little effect.

With the coming of peace, Spears returned home and was given a baronetcy in 1953. He retained a great zest for life and continued to write, lecture and travel. In 1964 he took part in *The Great War*, a major television documentary containing eye-witness accounts of some of the crucial points of the conflict. And shortly before his death in 1974, he was again in front of the cameras and microphones, this time talking about the momentous events as France fell in 1940 for a series on the twentieth century's second global conflict, *The World at War*. At his funeral, which took place at St Margaret's church, Westminster, a fanfare was provided by buglers of the 11th Hussars, the unit which had played such a great part in his life and for which he had done so much in return.

And perhaps the last word should go this remarkable man, for in one of the appendices to his book *Liaison 1914*, when talking of the heroines he had helped he put forward an idea which sadly has yet to be realized but which this book may perhaps help to bring about somewhere fitting, as we mark the centenary of these events. He wrote:

Only one thing remains to be done. I hope that somewhere in England, if not a statue, at least a tablet commemorating these fine deeds will be erected one day. These women deserve the honour, and we owe it to them and ourselves. To keep their memory green will be to perpetuate the finest trait known to human nature. 'For greater love hath no man than this.'

Acknowledgements

Many thanks are due for the assistance we have received during the research and writing of this book and we would like to give credit to those who have helped us along the way.

John's wife Kath was the one who first spotted the testimonial without which this book would have never been written. Thanks to Kath also for her valued research, enthusiasm and support.

Victor's wife, Diane Piuk's patience and computer skills have been much tested again in recovering lost bits of text, putting up with the cursing and the lost rare days we used to have out and about or at the seaside. Normal service will now be restored (though probably still with some cursing).

Of great help here in France have been the staff at the library and archive at Le Cateau, particularly Monsieur Alain Simon in the archives there who offered much information we would never have unearthed without him and who has taken great interest in the project.

Renowned author, friend and all-round good egg Richard van Emden has also been an early and steadfast supporter and was good enough to read a draft of the manuscript, make many helpful suggestions and give some good pointers using his seemingly encyclopaedic knowledge of the National Archives at Kew.

Thanks too to Tom McDade for information on the Vandeleurs and Terry Mackenzie from the Cameronians' Museum in Lanark for assistance during the early days of research.

A big thank you to the grandchildren of David & Aimée, especially Glen Cruickshank, Lisa Breakwell and Lynne Geoghagen for family stories and photographs.

Finally, many thanks to the editorial team of Pen & Sword for their advice, help and guidance during the publishing process.

Permissions have been sought for any material which may be covered by copyright but if any infringement has occurred it is our responsibility and will be amended in any future edition.

Bibliography

Books

Ascoli, D., *Mons Star*, Book Club Associates, 1982

Baynes, J., *Morale. A Study of Men and Courage*, Leo Cooper, 1987

Bird, A., *Gentlemen, We Will Stand and Fight*, The Crowood Press, 2009

Borden, M., *The Forbidden Zone*, Hesperus, 2008

Bloem, Captain W., *The Advance from Mons*, Tandem, 1967

Cave, N. & Sheldon, J., *Le Cateau*, Pen & Sword, 2008

Clark-Kennedy, A. E. (ed), *Old Contemptible Harry Beaumont*, Hutchinson, 1967

Cusack, J., *Scarlet Fever*, Cassell, 1972

Darrow, Margaret H., *French Women and the First World War*, Berg, 2000

Edmonds, Brigadier-General Sir J. E. (ed), *Official History of the War 1914*, Battery Press, 1996

Gibson, E. & Ward, K., *Courage Remembered*, HMSO Books, 1989

Longworth, P., *The Unending Vigil*, Secker & Warburg, 1967

Macdonald, L., *1914. The Days of Hope*, Penguin, 1987

McIntyre, B., *A Foreign Field,* Harper Collins, 2002

McPhail, H., *The Long Silence*, I.B.Taoris, 2001

Messenger, C., *Call to Arms. The British Army 1914–18*, Weidenfeld & Nicolson, 2005

Money Barnes, Major R., *The British Army of 1914*, Seeley, 1968

Royle, T., *The Flowers of the Forest. Scotland & the First World War*, Birlinn, 2007

Spears, Major General Sir E., *Liaison 1914*, Windmill Press, 1930

Terraine, J., (ed), *General Jack's Diary 1914–1918*, Eyre & Spottiswoode, 1964

Terraine J., *Mons. The Retreat to Victory*, Leo Cooper, 1991

Van Emden, R., *Prisoners of the Kaiser*, Pen & Sword, 2000

Westlake, R., *The British Army of 1914*, Spellmount, 2005

Westlake, R., *British Battalions in France & Belgium 1914*, Leo Cooper, 1997

Westlake, R., *British Battalions on the Somme*, Leo Cooper, 1994
Yarnall, J., *Barbed Wire Disease. British & German POWs 1914–19*,
  Spellmount, 2011

Magazines and journals
'Behind the Lines. The Story of the Iron Twelve', Professor Hedley
  Malloch, *The Western Front Association*
Daily Telegraph, editions February to April 1927
Journal Caudry-Cambresis, 17 April 1927
Sous Leur Griffes 1914–18, Oscar Masson (ed), Cambrai
The Covenanter (regimental magazine of the Cameronians)
'The Secret of the Mill', Herbert Walton, *World Wide Magazine*, 1928

Other media
www.cwgc.org The website of the Commonwealth War Graves
  Commission
Soldiers Who Died in the Great War. CD-ROM produced by the
  Naval and Military Press
The National Archives, London, WO 161 files